Intelligence Thoughts:
Developments in Iran, Iraq,
Afghanistan

Intelligence Thoughts: Developments in Iran, Iraq, Afghanistan

Howard P. Hart

ISBN 978-0-557-52746-5

Disclaimer

All statements of fact, opinion, or analysis expressed are those of the author and do not reflect the official positions or views of the CIA or any other U.S. Government agency. Nothing in the contents should be construed as asserting or implying U.S. Government authentication of information or Agency endorsement of the author's views. This material has been reviewed by the CIA to prevent the disclosure of classified information.

Preamble

I wrote the articles in this book between May 2009 and May 2010, a period during which many major events took place in Iraq, Afghanistan and Iran: we are in the midst of wars in the first two countries; and, as regards Iran, issues involving that country's internal stability, its efforts to acquire nuclear weapons, and its hostile external machinations, have considerable impact on the Unites States.

These are complex situations in areas that are unfamiliar and unintelligible to most Americans.

I wrote with several objectives in mind: to provide background information intended to assist a reader to make sense out of some very esoteric situations; and, based on my own long exposure to the area, to analyze and comment on developments and possible outcomes. I have tried to approach these issues from a dispassionate perspective - not as commentator with a political bias. I was trained to observe, analyze and report on events as they <u>are</u>, carefully avoiding the temptation to "spin" information to support any given policy or agenda.

The one blanket exception to my policy of objectivity is that I <u>do</u> write from an American perspective, meaning that I have a specific bias towards what I believe are the best interests of the United States. Further, where I have made specific criticisms, comments or recommendations, I have been careful to flag such commentary as my <u>personal opinions and views</u>.

Every item reported as fact in my writing comes from open, unclassified sources.

A final note: while many people claim to be "experts" on developments in these areas (and a few who make such claims actually <u>are</u> careful long-time students of the area, <u>and</u> have had the absolutely necessary extensive time "on the ground",) No one, including myself, has ever or will ever "get it all right." As one Wise Man said, developments in "the Middle East often defy logic". I think that is the One Great Truth about the Middle East.

Table of Contents

Saturday, May 2, 2009

Observations on Obama's Middle Eastern Policy

I feel vaguely like a traitor making the suggestions I make below. Specifically, I am hugely conscious of the enormous sacrifice our military has made thus far in both Iraq and Afghanistan – and truly hate acknowledging that the blood spilt so far - theirs - has mostly been in vain. On the other hand I am now confident that Obama is not a "war president", and has neither the courage nor the intention of fighting this war the way it should be fought. A President who will not stand up to our ostensible allies in the EU and NATO and forcefully and insistently make the case for their support is, I think, hardly likely to stand up when things get even more difficult.

I also think that Congress, and the Great Liberal Majority, however somnolent they now are, will eventually pull the rug out from under our soldiers, and perhaps from him, just as they did to George Bush. So ... better to cut our future military losses than to ask for more blood from our military without giving them the total, all-out support that any country owes its warriors. So, in fact, I feel that I am standing up for them.

I can only speculate why Obama has chosen to act as he has. Certainly our military knows the history of the past years in Iraq and the dangers of fighting in Afghanistan without guaranteed all-out support from the nation. Being our military, they saddle up to do what they are told. And they do it when they know full well that they do not and will not have their country's full manpower, moral and material support behind them.

Iraq

Candidate Obama made it very clear that he wanted out of Iraq – post haste. Pressed, he allowed that he would withdraw in no more than 16 months. Elected, that date has been pushed further and further away. We have now been given a "date certain" that is roughly 2 YEARS away. I also note that - without public acknowledgment of the success of the Bush "surge" plan (which was virulently opposed by the Congressional Left Wing) - he repeatedly says that things are going rather well in Iraq. In fact, this has become a fundamental justification for extending our stay.

I do NOT understand the Left Wing's silence on this absolute betrayal of one of his most important campaign promises. Since the Iraq War was the campaign issue, and certainly the issue that most exercised the Left Wing in vilifying Bush, I simply do not get the crashing post-election silence. Where did all the Left Wing wisdom on the "horrible mistake/tragedy/we need to get the hell out of the sandpit" go? The headline appears to be "Obama Adoration ExcU.S.es Abandonment of Major Campaign Promise – Liberals Silent".

Moving from that issue, we need to address the wisdom of the policy itself. Despite this extension, Iraqis, Iranians, and the rest of the Middle East do not expect the U.S. to remain there "long enough" – which in fact is "indefinitely" – to put things in some semblance of order. In their eyes, the Iraq War (in terms of the U.S.) is over. After many years in and dealing with the ME, I can safely assert that one of the few "truths" about the place is that in struggles like this, what matters most to the individual is not ideology or religion, but that he winds up on the "winning side." Survival first, all else is secondary. For Iraqis of every stripe, this means making use of the time until the Gringos Go Home to position themselves to be in the "right place and on the right side" when the final U.S. departure comes, and in the Middle East two years is a very short time.

As a practical matter, this policy means that our GI's will remain in Iraq – and continue to be killed there – long enough for the sides to continue to form up for the inevitable internal civil war that will follow our departure. And it gives Iran more than enough time, by continuing and expanding its extensive covert activities in Iraq, to prepare to assume hegemony over a very large chunk of the country. Put another way, our guys will continue dying for absolutely no reason whatever, and we will continue to pour money down a rat hole.

And that appears to be okay with the Left. I find that shocking.

I supported the invasion of Iraq, where there WERE, O Unbelievers, weapons of mass destruction, which Saddam had worlds of time to move out of the country. (To where, we ask? That will soon become a nice new problem.) I did not in my wildest dreams foresee the willful arrogance and stupidity of the Rumsfeld/Bush team that led to the occupation and pacification operations we have so long been involved in. It absolutely grieves me to opine, after so many American deaths, that we have no choice but to cut our losses and leave. Soonest. Yes, the consequences will be serious for the U.S., but they will be whether we stay two more years or not. That, I believe, is the bottom line.

Afghanistan

Obama has decided to radically ramp-up American military strength, and to spend a whole bunch more on "development assistance" - without even token support from our NATO allies. (Please note how his recent pleas to the EU/NATO for increased support in Afghanistan were absolutely and utterly rejected. And he made no effort to press the Europeans on the subject.)

Obama plans to have about 80,000 American troops in Afghanistan by next year - up from roughly 38,000. While our forces are infinitely better trained, equipped, motivated, skilled and supported than were the Soviets that is simply not enough men. Just as in Iraq, political considerations will dictate how many men we can actually put into the country, and even with the "Obama Aura" I doubt our force level could be raised to what I estimate is a number approaching 150,000 combatants.

Obama has chosen to abandon one war to fight an even larger one. Again, the Left Wing, both in Congress and the country at large, is silent and apparently accepting.

Having spent some years running a war in that country against 130,000 Soviet troops, plus another 40,000 communist Afghan Army forces, I have some claim to an informed opinion on our prospects there.

In brief: this effort will fail, at a terrible cost in American blood and treasure. It should NOT go forward.

Why?

1. Afghanistan is a HUGE area, which, except for lines on a map, has never met the basic definition of being a "country". It is no more a country than is Europe, Urals to London, or the former Yugoslavia. Worse, it has no repeat no history of any kind of effective centralized government - in fact the very concept of such a government runs counter

to almost every Afghan's basic instincts. To most Afghans, the best government is NO government. It is populated in large part by people who love to fight and kill: killing foreign "Unbelievers" (whether Soviet or American) is particularly attractive, and we made good use of this fact in supporting the Afghan insurgency. Or by people who, after 29 years of warfare and turmoil, just want the fighting to end, no matter who wins. It is, and always has been, ungovernable. In and around it are enemy forces that are savage, intractably opposed to the ideas and concepts we are trying to foster; well armed; derive huge financial support from opium production; and have safe havens in both Pakistan and Iran.

In my opinion, unless Obama intends to fight a war there indefinitely, increasing both our military presence and civil aid, and expects that he can get our country and Congress to go along with him well into the future, there is no chance of "victory". So, once again, and with great reluctance, I submit we must withdraw. Again: witness Vietnam or Iraq.

2. Pakistan is an utterly failed state, with a growing radical Islamic population determined to destroy - by any means - the existing government and its "American connection." Given its internal stresses, largely initiated by Muslim radicals who are supported by the mullahs and power-hungry politicians - and opposed by even more feckless "moderates" – it is doubtful that Pakistan can or will remain an ally/base for the logistics operations that are an absolute requirement for U.S. to fight a major war in Afghanistan. Further, to assume that Pakistan will tacitly continue to allow drone aircraft to attack enemy targets inside Pakistan is equally unrealistic.

    a) Our entire effort depends on using Pakistan as a secure supply route, moving materiel from its seaport at Karachi to the Afghan border and into the country. Those convoys are already under attack, and will probably become increasingly insecure, perhaps unusable. It is logistically impossible to fight a major war in Afghanistan using air supply alone.

b)   I need not belabor how the country's Frontier Province, which constitutes the entire border with Afghanistan, is totally beyond the control of the Pakistan Army and has long served as a safe haven for anti-U.S. fighters. Osama bin Laden and the Taliban have been there in relative safety for years. Within the past week the pathetic Pakistani Government, under armed attack by "radical elements" which the Army was unable to defeat, has officially created a safe haven for Taliban/al-Qaeda forces in one small but easily defended portion of the Frontier: poor little Swat, which is not and never has been a hotbed of radical Islamic fervor. This marks, for the first time, the explicit surrender of Pakistani territory to Taliban/al-Qaeda forces. That would seem to be an unpleasant portent of things to come.

c)   Iran, already providing covert support to "bad Afghans", can be expected to increase that support. I submit that Iran will soon become as important a supply/training safe haven for enemy Afghans as Pakistan was for U.S. in fighting the Soviets.

So ... once again, where is the Left Wing? Since the Left absolutely controls the Congress, its Main Man is President, and Republicans are reduced to quarrelsome insignificance, only the Left can provide meaningful reasoned discussion and/or opposition to the new war that Obama has chosen for U.S. to fight – and fight alone. My guess is that, once again, the "Obama Aura" simply blinds Liberals from even serioU.S.ly questioning this policy.

That is leading U.S. to a national tragedy – a la Iraq, or Vietnam.

Monday, May 11, 2009

Funding for Nuclear Detection Eliminated?

In his most recent announcement of "cuts" to the Federal Budget - cuts which amount to a breath-taking one-half of 1 percent of next year's budget - President Obama included, to quote from a Washington Post article of 8 May 2009, the elimination of "new spending to buy advanced-generation sensors to detect nuclear bombs of radioactive materials at U.S. ports and borders, a Bush priority that has had technical problems."

I consider this to be an appallingly short-sighted decision and, unless it is reversed, a very real potential threat to our national security.

My reasoning is as follows: at least two countries (North Korea and Iran) either have or soon will have nuclear weapons. Another country, Pakistan, which has nuclear weapons, is a political and economic disaster, and is now in the throes of a massive challenge by radical Islamic militants. While the U.S. has been helping Pakistan beef-up the physical security of its nuclear arsenal to defend against precisely this threat, in my opinion there is a serious medium to long-term threat that those militants would be able to steal or otherwise gain control of one or more weapons.

Having a nuclear "device" is one thing; delivering it to a distant target country quite another. Note: I use the word "device" intentionally. "Conventional" nuclear-armed countries package their nuclear weapons as bombs and/or missile warheads because they have aircraft and/or missile delivery systems. Crowding the components for a nuclear weapon into a bomb or warhead package requires considerable sophistication.

This does NOT, however, mean that countries (or terrorist organizations) that lack a long-range delivery system and/or the technical sophistication to cram the components into a neat package are not a threat to the United States - or Israel and other potential target countries. Quite the opposite: freed from the size and other constraints imposed by bomb/warhead design, a perfectly effective nuclear device (think a bomb in a crate) can be carried to its target destination by commercial carrier - e.g., as falsely manifested cargo aboard a ship or cargo aircraft.

It is important to note that attacking the U.S. in this manner effectively hides the identity of the attackers, and gives anonymity and plausible denial to enemy states that could have sponsored the attack, as well as to "stateless" terrorist organizations. In other words, it makes impossible any threat of reprisal by the U.S. - there is no "deterrence factor."

Based on my years in the intelligence business - including much time spent trying to assist U.S. Government agencies identify and intercept major shipments of narcotics into the country by "commercial means" - I am confident that inserting a nuclear weapon/device into the U.S. by this means is very doable. At the same time it is completely impracticable to physically inspect every one of the hundreds of thousands of cargo containers that arrive by sea in U.S. ports each year. Nor is it possible to physically inspect all arriving air cargos. By definition, this means that our only potentially effective defense at our ports of entry is the deployment of highly sophisticated sensors - which should also be put in place at key overseas ports of origin.

I am sure that the design of such sensors is very difficult. That said I believe that not to press forward with a major national scientific effort to develop these sensors is naive, irrational, and poses a major long-term threat to our national security. Just imagine the consequences of a nuclear explosion that originates on a ship in Long Beach or New York or ...

This issue transcends party politics, and certainly does not merit being dismissed in a token budget-cutting exercise. I urge everyone to contact their Congressional representatives to demand that scientific work on this problem not only continue, but be expanded on a priority basis.

Wednesday, May 27, 2009

Iran's Nuclear Weapons Program

In view of many concerns regarding Iran's nuclear weapons program, I thought it worth bringing the National Intelligence Estimate (NIE) of November 2007 to your attention.

That Estimate, which was based on intelligence available through October 2007, is now almost two years old. It states (with "moderate confidence") that IF Iran resumed its weapons program (after November 2007) the earliest that it could produce enough fissile material (enriched uranium) for a weapon is late 2009 into 2010. Both dates are soon upon us.

Those amongst us who have always wanted to try their hands at "estimative" (i.e., predictive) intelligence might find amusement in reviewing the responsible world press for clues as to what course of action Iran has taken since the fall of 2007.

The NIE can be found at the following URL: http:// blogs.abcnews.com /politicalradar/2007/12/nie-report-iran.html

Tuesday, June 16, 2009

Assessment Iran

No one in the world, least of all the Iranian people or government, knows what the outcome of the current political crisis in that country will be.

The parallels between what happened in Iran in 1978-79, when the Khomeini revolution against the Shah ignited and succeeded, and what is happening in Iran today are extraordinary.

We know that Iran's religious oligarchy and President Ahmadinejad did not expect the intensity of public protest in the wake of the recent election. Whether or not the election was rigged – as it probably was – the protest demonstrations have proven that significant numbers of Iranians are anti-Ahmadinejad and are challenging the authority of the theocratic oligarchy. Demonstrators appear to be well-educated students and business people of the middle class in Tehran. As far as I can tell the lower classes have not as yet emerged to support the protests. In effect, the young intelligencia and the middle class city worker have found common cause, yet we have not yet heard from the bulk of the population, particularly in the provincial cities.

What is at issue over the next several days is whether the protestors, in the wake of an extraordinary concession by Iran's Guardian Council – an agreement to recount some ballots from last week's Presidential election – will continue their major demonstrations. While the Guardian Council has expressly stated that it will not void the election as a result of this review, I believe the action, like it or not, will encourage the demonstrators to believe they have won a signal victory: which I suspect will encourage more anti-regime activity. The concession is clearly an attempt to defuse what the mullahs have come to recognize as a bona fide threat to their continued sovereignty. Despite the Council's claim to the contrary, the concession opens the door to the possibility that Ahmadinejad's election can be voided: a huge victory for the protestors.

If the demonstrations continue at the same or larger level, and spread to major provincial cities, I believe the regime is likely to take more violent actions to suppress them in an attempt to retain its power and authority. Should the demonstrations quickly taper off I suspect the mullahs will believe they have largely defused the situation – and probably will have.

It is interesting to note that President Ahmadinejad has elected to leave the country for a meaningless conference in Russia. This after having indicated he would not attend it because of the disturbances in the wake of his reelection. I read this as an indicator that the religious oligarchy is prepared to let loose the "defenders" of the status quo: elements of the Revolutionary Guard and the paramilitary religious police - The Basij. I say this because if violent repressive actions are taken against further major demonstrations, Ahmadinejad's absence will enable him to claim that he was not involved.

As we watch this play out, the next days and weeks are critical. We know that Iran's economic problems are enormous and affect all levels of Iranian society except the very rich and the mullah class. This provides fertile grounds for revolutionary upheaval. The entrenched power base in Iran: the oligarchy, the Revolutionary Guards, and all those who directly profit from the current political and economic situation, are likely to go to extremes to protect and maintain their power. Hence, if large demonstrations continue, and if the current class of protestors are joined in large numbers by the "lower" classes – always the traditional source of support for the theocracy – the threat level as perceived by the government will rise exponentially.

One of the major differences between the revolution of 1978-79 and this crisis is communications. In the anti-Shah revolution all that was available to the Shah's opponents to fan country-wide protests were telephones. The leaders of that revolution had to depend upon the BBC to spread the word of major demonstrations and protests: The Khomeini people simply told BBC reporters that there would be a huge demonstration in Tehran or Esfahan, etc., on a given day. BBC would dutifully announce the coming demonstrations and the crowds turned up.

Today's internet, cell phones, Twitter, E-mails, Blogs, and Face Book have greatly facilitated the protestors' ability to immediately spread information and foment wider protests. The other benefit of today's internet tools is that news of events can be spread quickly within the country, thus defeating the government's strong efforts to suppress the dissemination of information. The mullahs are well aware of that. If the Iranian political scene is radically transformed, it may be the first time the internet has made possible a revolution.

My assessment: a conservative analysis of the issues operating in Iran today would be that it is too soon to tell whether a major upheaval will take place in Iran. I am, however, willing to stick my neck out after years of Iran watching, and say that my instinct is that the "reform"/"protest" movement will grow and force President Ahmadinejad out. While it will not terminate the role of the religious oligarchy and the Revolutionary Guard, it will bring a much greater degree of democracy into the country's political system, and represent a major upheaval in Iran.

Tuesday, June 16, 2009

Iran Crisis: Mullah Manipulation of Communication Channels

In an article I circulated a few hours ago (***Assessment: Iran***) I noted that the many communications channels that the Internet provides (e.g., Twitter, YouTube, Facebook, email, blogs, etc.) are clearly playing an important role in assisting opposition elements transmit information within and outside of Iran.

I think that it is worth noting that while the Internet can be of enormous assistance to the opposition in fanning and sustaining protest activity, it is very much a double-edged sword. Those same channels can be used - and no doubt are being used - by the Government in a variety of ways to attack and defeat the opposition.

For example, the Government can originate messages purporting to come from "legitimate" opposition elements as a way to identify and entrapping dissidents, and to sow confusion and uncertainty in their ranks. In intelligence jargon, this is "false flagging" to misinform, identify, entrap and make these channels suspect to the dissidents.

And, of course, since every computer has a unique IP number, Government security forces can examine anti-government messages sent on individual computers and very often use their IP addresses to identify the senders.

Friday, June 19, 2009

Assessment Iran II

Developments in Iran are building to a rapid climax. Ayatollah Khamenei's speech on Friday, 19 June, made clear that the religious oligarchy as led by him will not reverse the election, nor will it tolerate further demonstrations. The call for a mass demonstration by Moussavi supporters on Saturday, 20 June, is therefore clearly a major challenge to the authority of both the Government and the clerical oligarchy. It will be interesting to see if the demonstration actually takes place, and, if it does, whether the Government will react with more force than it has yet chosen to exert. Developments over the next 24 hours will probably define the outcome of Moussavi's protest movement.

It is important to realize that the opposition is not, repeat not, attempting to overthrow the Islamic Republic. There have been no demands to alter the basic fabric of the Republic: the protests have been entirely focused on charges of "fixing" the election of President Ahmadinejad. Moussavi is hardly a liberal, so the demonstrators are not calling for radical political change. The opposition is not even challenging the already fraudulent and undemocratic means of candidate selection, much less the entire electoral/governing process.

In his convoluted Friday speech Ayatollah Khamenei seemed to regard the present protests as a threat to the entire structure of the Islamic Republic, and it appears that he, at least, views the protests as far more threatening than a squabble over the recent election.

Comment: Khamenei is a relic of the past, whose mind may not be grasping present realities. In many small ways his speech seemed to be more appropriate for a time before the overthrow of the Shah. I suspect that more than anything his subconscious focus, given many years of clerical impotence under the Shah, is on maintaining the national sovereignty of the senior clergy.

Therein lays the threat of a widening social rupture. If Khamenei and the Council of Guardians had chosen to throw out the election results and hold another election, which one thinks they could have done gracefully, probably winning support for clerical rule in the process; it is very probable that the protest movement would have immediately collapsed. It appears that he and a majority of "establishment" mullahs (as well as President Ahmadinejad) have rejected this course of action, thus escalating the crisis.

Fragmentary reporting from Iran indicates that the protestors in Tehran are now a mix of the lower and middle classes. What is happening in Iran's provincial cities is basically unknown, but it has long been the rule that as goes Tehran, so goes the country. The participation by the student literati, middle class business and government types, and, apparently, significant representation by the lower middle class is a particular threat to the government.

Tonight is a bad night in Tehran. Moussavi's people, now faced with a specific order not to rally, must be struggling about whether to risk the demonstration. On the other side there are major splits within the clerical oligarchy, and a number of senior mullahs have already condemned the election results. I suspect much hangs on what tack former President Rafsanjani, who hates President Ahmadinejad, elects to take. Thus far Rafsanjani has apparently been at least tacitly supporting Moussavi, and it is alleged that he has been working the mullah crowd in Qom to throw President Ahmadinejad to the dogs. Ahmadinejad is probably in favor of stepping up repressive action, and he controls the thugs of the Basij who have so far been responsible for the violence perpetrated against the demonstrators.

Comment: As always in Iran, conspiracy theories abound: one is that Rafsanjani, defeated by Ahmadinejad in the 2005 Presidential election, is actually quietly masterminding the entire protest movement in order to remove Ahmadinejad from office. As rumors go, this is not a bad one. If Rafsanjani either chooses - or is forced by his peers - to support a hard line/repressive approach, the consequences to Moussavi's supporters could be grave. If he does not, rifts in the clerical establishment could dramatically widen.

Tactically speaking, if the Government has decided to take actions against Saturday's now forbidden rally it has several courses of action. It can allow the protestors to arrive at the specified rally location and deal with the crowds there - where its options range from mild scuffles, clerical condemnation, etc., OR, a la Tiananmen Square, it can arrange for some real violence. Alternatively, it can, beginning tonight, harass and block movement towards the rallying point, thus preventing a large assembly of people. The question is what level of violence - if any - will the Government choose to exercise?

Saturday, July 4, 2009

Iran Strikes Back - What to do?

Iranian ruling authorities have suppressed the most virulent and threatening anti-regime protests since the Islamic "Republic" was established thirty years ago. The demonstrations have been shut down by the clerical regime's willingness to display and use massive force: no urban Iranian can be in doubt that the regime's very large security forces are sufficiently loyal to the mullahs to unleash a blood bath. The protest movement made absolutely clear to the world that democracy is a fiction in Iran, and that the clerical oligarchy will take any actions, no matter how violent, against its own citizens in order to remain in power.

Iran, however, has been irrevocably changed by the events of the past several weeks, and these changes will have both enormous internal consequences and very significant effects on Iran's dealings with the United States and the rest of the world. That is the subject of this writing.

Iran has by all measures been internationally humiliated and embarrassed. To counter what has become a terrible "image" problem, I believe that the regime will take steps to demonstrate that Iran remains a powerful and important player on the world stage. To this end I expect that in the wake of the protests we will see two major actions regarding Iran's external relations. The first will be even greater determination rapidly to develop nuclear weapons. In the leadership's view nothing would more quickly draw attention away from the regime's clear failure to deal with the Iranian people, and "restore" its international image, than an announcement that Iran has nuclear weapons.

Second, we should expect greatly increased clandestine Iranian involvement in Iraq: activities designed to destabilize Iraq's fragile government as the U.S. begins the process of military disengagement. A subservient Iraq has long been a goal of Iran's clerical oligarchy and of its civilian sycophants – read President Ahmadinejad. Given the already volatile and shaky nature of the "new" Iraq, the removal of U.S. troops will provide greatly increased opportunities to intervene in Iraq in order to destroy that country's nascent democratic political system and bring large parts of the country under de facto Iranian control.

If I am correct in these two judgments the difficulties faced by the United States in the area will be radically increased. Any chance for a meaningful dialogue between President Obama and President Ahmadinejad disappeared in the streets of Tehran.

This takes us to the question of what possible actions the U.S. might take to counter these Iranian moves. Even if President Obama believes that Iran's acquisition of nuclear weapons would represent an extraordinary and real danger to Middle Eastern and world stability, and if he is prepared to provide world leadership to suppress this Iranian threat, he has few options.

As regards the nuclear threat, there is no repeat no way that Iran's nuclear facilities could *with certainty* be destroyed by U.S. air strikes. (The same holds true for air strikes by the Israelis, even though Israel arrogantly tends to suggest that it could do the deed.) I say this because I doubt we have sufficiently good intelligence to ensure that we have identified every necessary target, and because it is extraordinarily difficult to destroy "hardened" underground facilities, which I assume the Iranians have had the forethought to construct.

One could argue that massive "surgical" air strikes that did *not* destroy *all* the crucial components of Iran's nuclear structure would still serve to significantly delay Iran's march toward nuclear weapons. This is probably true, but this approach has its own negative consequences. First, it probably would *serve* the clerical regime's interests by unleashing a wave of popular nationalist support for the mullahs – and pull the rug out from under the reform movement. There is also the fact that U.S. air strikes against Iran would, by the nature of things in the Middle East, no doubt produce a massive anti-U.S. reaction at a time when the new U.S. Administration is attempting to address the Israeli-Palestinian problem.

As regards increased Iranian activity to destabilize Iraq, there is as a practical matter no way to effectively block such actions, particularly given the rolling draw down of U.S. troop strength in Iraq. I have sadly concluded that non-Kurdish Iraq, in the near-term and despite the thousands of American war dead, will become a radical, unstable Iranian supported disaster.

I believe that Iran will also greatly increase its support for armed anti-U.S. elements in Afghanistan. This will be the subject of a separate piece.

So…what to do? If the option of U.S. military action (air strikes) is rejected, it would appear that the only way to *force* Iran to abandon its nuclear weapons program, and, perhaps, its potentially increased intervention in Iraq, would be a massive and effective economic blockade – similar to that successfully established against Libya. Given the events of the past weeks in Iran the EU, with some strong American prodding, might be willing to take the necessary steps to isolate Iran. Middle Eastern countries and Japan would also have to be pressured to go along with this plan of action. China will do nothing in support of such activity, and the Russians would probably also refuse to participate. It is likely, however, that even if China and Russia do not lend a hand, a total economic embargo of Iran would have a good chance of success.

Comment: It seems to me that Iran has now assumed the same role in Mr. Obama's presidency that it did with Jimmy Carter's. In Carter's case his refusal to take immediate, overt military action against Iran in the wake of capturing the U.S. Embassy, cost the United States enormous embarrassment and cost Carter his presidency. Jimmy Carter proved that the "come let us reason together" approach to a world which sometimes does not play fair did not work. The Iranian clerical regime remembers well how it humiliated and humbled the United States in the Carter era. It will be interesting to see whether President Obama pays attention to the lessons of the Carter-Iran imbroglio. President Obama is in the difficult position – made even more difficult by recent events in Iran – of having to choose whether to accept the fairly near-term emergence of Iran as a nuclear power, or to exercise American influence and power to the utmost in order to attempt to block that from happening.

Monday, July 6, 2009

Assessment Iran III

My July 4, 2009, article discussing possible responses to the situation in Iran asserted that massive economic sanctions against Iran would be the U.S.'s only viable option in an effort to disrupt Iran's obvious efforts to obtain nuclear weapons. And, coincidentally, to assist that country to shake off the clerical despotism that now rules it.

One highly qualified observer responded to the article with the comment that economic sanctions of the size that would be necessary to work towards the above ends could be a double edged sword. In effect, he suggested that sanctions could prompt the Iranian people to rally behind the clerical regime. That is a possibility. I think, however, that it is far more likely that the majority of the population, led by the millions of people who took part in the recent demonstrations, would see such sanctions for what they are: a Western (or even just an American) effort to bring down a despotic clerical regime. And welcome them. Sanctions would cripple an already shaky economy, and the gamble would be that "the people" would not accept the regime's calls to tough it out – and instead lead to major riots in the streets. In that event the clerics and their thugs would be forced to decide whether to resort again to bloody repressive tactics – probably on a much larger scale – in order to "restore calm". My belief is that if the junta opted for really wide-spread violence in response to major demonstrations, the regime would fall.

Here are a few additional thoughts.

The now silenced protests have, among other things, resulted in the grim exposure of the absolute power of Iran's senior clergy. In the wake of the Khomeini Revolution, Iran's system of government was carefully crafted to keep absolute power in the hands of religious zealots. The past months have revealed with astonishing clarity just how this unrestrained clerical power operates behind the fiction of an "elected" president and parliament. Further, that when circumstances threaten the clerical oligarchy, the ruling clerics turn to their

Revolutionary Guard and Basij thugs to enforce their dictates. The Iranian government, as represented both by the Grand Ayatollah Khamenei (the "Islamic side" of government) and his sycophantic President Ahmadinejad and Majlis (Parliament) (the "Republican" side) have, in responding to legal public protests that appeared to the Establishment to threaten their absolute rule, unleashed security organizations that exactly mirror Hitler's SS and SA "Brown Shirts"- the Nazi Party tools of repression. (On close examination it is astonishing to see how closely the system of governance established by Ayatollah Khomeini matches the organization and methods of Hitler's Germany.)

The events of the past month or so have been implicitly acknowledged by the regime to represent the most significant and dangerous threat to Khomeini's Islamic form of government since its inception in 1979. An astonishing series of events have demonstrated the extraordinary divide between popular will and sovereignty and the ruling junta, and the grim and often bloody determination of the ruling clergy and its vassal "civilian" enforcers to shut down any challenge to their rule and authority. One such event was the Friday prayer session on 26 June 2009, led by Ahmed Khatami, one of the most senior of the ruling Ayatollahs, who declared that "those who are opposing the ruling regime were at war with God," and should be "dealt with without mercy". Further, the Ayatollah, speaking for the Grand Ayatollah and President Ahmadinejad, commanded: "Anybody who fights against the Islamic system or the leaders of Islamic society, fight him until complete destruction." Khatami was in fact invoking God's retribution upon any Iranian who challenges the regime.

These statements were both clear and forceful threats to the populace by the highest level of the ruling clerical oligarchy and clerical justification for bloody repression in the name of Allah.

As the world watched Iran's post-election protests we saw large elements of the citizenry focus solely on the issue of a manipulated election. At no point did the protestors directly criticize the clerical regime or its vassal President Ahmadinejad. I believe this was a subtle and intentional strategy designed to avoid direct confrontation with both clerical and presidential powers over the much more fundamental issues of Iran's sham democracy. More focused criticism would have resulted in immediate and savage repression. In effect, the protestors hung their complaints on what was manifestly a rigged election rather than taking the "government" head-on. After crowd suppression became more violent, we did start to see occasional signs reading "death to the dictator". Who is the "dictator"? In my view those signs were specifically directed at Grand Ayatollah Khamenei and President Ahmadinejad, and represented the first expression of direct criticism of Iran's government. I think that the regime recognized that the protestors were not just complaining of a rigged election but were attacking the greater issue of a sham democracy controlled by the clergy and its "civilian" minions.

It is important to understand that the clergy are not a monolithic block united in their resolve to dominate every aspect of Iran's political, religious and economic life. From the very establishment of the government structure designed by Ayatollah Khomeini significant elements of Iran's senior clergy disagreed with Khomeini's assertion of clerical omnipotence. For the most part, however, these dissidents remained silent. The recent protests have, however, clearly surfaced the divisions within the clergy: on the one side are the hard liners determined to maintain complete clerical domination, on the other are the clergy who believe the clerical establishment should not become involved in governing Iran.

Despite a highly effective government effort to shut-down both internal news reporting and communications between protestors, it was apparent that there was dissention within the clerical establishment. This split has in the past several days become more visible, and, I think, represents one of the most significant (and potentially threatening to the regime) developments in the wake of the protests. The most persuasive evidence of this internal tension surfaced in Cairo on July 4 2009 where it was reported that "the most important group of religious leaders in Iran", headquartered in Qom, disputed the election and called the new government illegitimate. (The New York Times, July 5, 2009, "Leading Clerics Defy Ayatollah on Disputed Iran Election".)

There could be no more threatening development for the regime than the emergence of significant and overt criticism of absolute clerical rule by important members of the clerical establishment. How the regime reacts to and manages divisions in the ranks of the senior clergy will play a great role in Iran's future. If, for example, the already alienated but repressed public believes these divisions are widespread I believe it will give renewed vigor to the anti-government movement.

It has not been widely noted that a large majority of Iran's nineteen Ayatollahs were deafeningly silent during the demonstrations – i.e., they did not speak up for the government when it was under very considerable stress. And that majority remains silent.

For the moment then it would seem that our best approach would be to move forward in an attempt to obtain broad support for economic sanctions. While this diplomatic effort, which would take some time, is underway, we should carefully watch developments in Iran – specifically to see whether the dissident clergy acts to bring about significant changes in Iran's governance.

Monday, July 6, 2009

Comment by Former Secretary of State Lawrence Eagleburger on Iran

Note: I received the following comments regarding my 6 July 2009 article on Iran from former Secretary of State Larry Eagleburger. I am sure that everyone who reads these comments and my article "knows" Larry, both from his days in the State Department and, since his retirement from Government, from his frequent guest appearances on various network news shows. Larry is a Great American and a patriot who speaks his mind.

I very much support your excellent analysis ("Iran Strikes Back - What to Do?") of where Iran is following the "upset" of the past several weeks. I do have comments on several points in your article, but they are not to be seen as criticisms. Rather, you know me and my proclivity for always trying to have the last word.

First, I note that someone has already suggested that the embargo you described in your article could lead to a hostile reaction in Iran. Of course it would - as would any other course of action (which you point out in your original piece). The issue is not whether if we act will it affect popular attitudes in Iran; rather it is can we find a means of forcing Iran to give up its nuclear weapons program THAT WILL WORK? If it is unlikely to succeed then it is not worth the costs, including giving rise to popular antagonism in Iran. I agree with you that the only available and supportable action that might succeed is an embargo of the kind you suggest. But the key word here is "supportable". As you point out, there are other possible courses of action, but they potentially carry with them unacceptable costs to U.S.

On the question of an embargo, I also agree that if we could engineer one that included most nations it could work. However, my friend, you have avoided the critical question: does this new administration of ours have the intestinal fortitude necessary to "persuade" others to join U.S. in an embargo? And, should we obtain agreement to establish that embargo, would we be ready to use force to assure its effectiveness? I understand your desire to remain above the debate on the President's strengths (if there are any) and weaknesses (too numerous to count?), but in the end a philosophical analysis must be viewed in the light of reality. And that reality is that the President of the United States has already demonstrated to friend and foe alike that he does not understand: a) the complexity of foreign affairs; b) that there are some very nasty people out there who only understand strength; c) that those nasty people are likely to judge our strength by watching the words and actions of the President.

My point, sir, is that to obtain broad agreement on an embargo would require a willingness to be tough with a number of nations, and I do not believe that President Obama has the toughness necessary to persuade others to agree to join in an embargo, much less to assure that it is observed if agreed to.

I am left, therefore, with the belief that Iran's ability to build a nuclear weapon will rest totally in Iran's hands; if it has the technical ability to build a weapon it will join the nuclear club. The timing I cannot predict, but that it will own a weapon is all but assured.

One final point: Your comments about the Carter-Obama similarities are correct, but remember that Carter had far more provocation in the seizure of our embassy and personnel than Obama has or will have. Thus, he has even less reason than Carter did to act.

Wednesday, July 8, 2009

Iran: Nuclear Timeline

In a 4 July 2009 posting on this blog I commented that from an intelligence perspective it is highly likely that Iran, in the wake of recent wide-scale domestic disturbances, would act to expedite its development of nuclear weapons.

In a Wall Street Journal article of 8 July, Adm Mike Mullen, Chairman of the Joint Chiefs of Staff, told a Washington audience that "the window is closing" on the time available to prevent Iran from making nuclear weapons. He further stated that Iran *"was likely just one to three years away from successfully building a nuclear weapon."* The Admiral also said the U.S. is also keeping "all options on the table...including, certainly, military options."

This is the first timeline that I have noted from a highly credible spokesman on Iran's nuclear weapons potential. I do not know whether Adm Mullen cleared his speech with the White House: whether he did or not is irrelevant, and I think that we should take his statement at face value. The time remaining for any attempt to take effective proactive steps to force Iran to abandon its nuclear program is very short, and the administration must decide immediately what path of action it will or will not take.

The present situation in North Korea provides a lesson that should not be ignored. Several U.S. administrations spent years, usually in fragile and thoroughly unsatisfactory association with other major Powers, to cajole, bribe, and threaten North Korea in an effort to stop that country's nuclear weapons program. The absolute failure of these efforts has been made crystal clear by that country's nuclear weapons testing and its successful development of large numbers of missiles. This suggests that anything less than direct military action *or* extremely restrictive sanctions will result in Iran's having its own nuclear arsenal in the near future.

Monday, July 20, 2009

Iraq: Ominous Portents

It has long been my view that unless the U.S. maintains a significant military presence in Iraq – perhaps for an additional 10 years – that country will quickly collapse into civil war. Saddam Hussein's Sunni minority (roughly 35%) controlled a Shia majority (roughly 63%) and a Kurdish minority (roughly 17%) by bloody and violent repression. The American-led invasion to destroy Saddam in 2003 was brilliantly successful and quickly achieved. This was immediately followed by the U.S.'s determination to establish – by force - and "leave behind" a stable democratically elected Iraqi national government. As the years of warfare in Iraq have proven, this strategic decision was arrogantly dismissive of the realities of Iraq's religious, political and cultural history, and led to over six years of costly indecisive fighting in Iraq. In the course of which our "coalition" allies dropped out, one by one. (The last remaining coalition combat force, 4,000 British troops, is now withdrawing and will not be replaced.) More than six years of extraordinary efforts by the U.S. and its allies to defeat a wide spectrum of anti-U.S. and anti-Iraqi governments militants – an effort which to date has claimed the lives of 4326 Americans (as of 18 July 2009) – have produced, at best, a stalemate.

Long heatedly debated in U.S. domestic politics, the political decision to exit Iraq was set in concrete with President Obama's 2008 election. The new President has decided on a phased withdrawal, rather than a precipitous pull-out, in order, presumably, to give the present Iraqi government limited continued U.S. military support – and time to solidify its position.

In his 27 February 2009 announcement of his plans to leave Iraq, President Obama stated that, "by 31 August 2010 our combat mission in Iraq will end". The first step in the exit strategy, apparently, was the withdrawal of our combat troops from Iraqi cities at the end of June 2009, at which time most of our forces retreated to desert camps. His second step was to order the removal of the majority of U.S. combat forces from Iraq *on a schedule which he did not enunciate*, but which he stated would be completed by 31 August 2010. His final step would be to leave a force of 35,000 – 50,000 personnel, who, according to the President, would stay in Iraq for an additional year – until August 2011. The mission of this residual force would be to train and advise the Iraqi security forces; protect American civilians (presumably American contractors and non-military government employees engaged in "nation building" and infrastructure repair); and to *hunt terrorist cells*.

How does this translate into numbers of troops? At peak strength the U.S. deployed approximately 142,000 soldiers: a peak that was reached as a result of the "surge" in troop strength (hotly contested by Congressional Democrats) made necessary by escalating insurgent attacks. A cut of two (of fourteen) combat brigades (totaling about 12,000 personnel) in the next few months will reduce U.S. troop strength to roughly 128,000 personnel. Again, we have not been given a time table for reducing the 128,000 over the next year to the 35,000 – 50,000 scheduled to remain in-country beginning in August 2010.

The shaky Shia-dominated Iraqi government chose to celebrate July 1 as a national holiday marking the withdrawal of American troops to desert encampments. The holiday ostensibly highlighted Iraq's self-declared ability to stand on its own, with primary responsibility for defending a "united" Iraq left in the hands of Iraqi government security forces.

There have been a number of developments over the past days that, I believe, have serious and ominous implications regarding the future of Iraq and the decline of the U.S. military presence in that country.

First, the Shia-led national government has in the past days issued a mandate to U.S. field commanders that Americans are to stop all "joint patrols" (i.e., Iraqi security forces operating *in conjunction* with U.S. troops) in Baghdad. Further, President Maliki has ordered that American supply convoys are to move only at night. These orders, if allowed to stand, will severely restrict the combat role and effectiveness of U.S. troops, while also a) denying U.S. troops the assistance provided by Iraqi soldiers who know the territory, and b) denying Iraqi units the desperately needed experience gained by fighting alongside U.S. soldiers. Surprised U.S. commanders are appealing these restrictions, which have the gravest implications for our ability to continue effectively to fight "insurgent" elements.

It is possible that these new restrictions are the result of an over-confident President Maliki's determination to prove that his government no longer needs immediate American military assistance.

However, since no sensible observer would consider the Iraqis prepared to provide security on their own, I suspect the restrictions are part of a larger plan by Maliki's Shia supporters to prepare for the struggle to ensure Shia dominance in post-U.S. Iraq. I believe that Maliki, by restricting American military activity, particularly in Baghdad, is moving to allow increased Shia militant activity. If this is the case, President Obama may in fact have to re-think whether U.S. troops should remain in Iraq for (even) as long as he now plans.

Second, there has recently been an escalation of attacks on U.S. forces by Shia militants, all of whom are supported by Iran's Revolutionary Guard by the provision of training, weapons and funds. Many of these groups are under the control of the infamous radical Shia cleric Moqtada al-Sadr, who demonstrated his strength by bringing terror to Baghdad and southern Iraq in 2006. In addition, we have noted a number of serious. Sunni suicide bombings in Shia areas, indicating that the Sunni's are increasing pressure on their Shia opponents. The smaller Sunni militias will probably not waste their resources in attacks on the Americans: they can leave that to the Shia, and will focus on their Shia enemies.

Third, in our 4 July 2009 article, "Iran Strikes Back", we made the following assertion: (In the wake of the recent unrest in Iran) *we should expect greatly increased clandestine Iranian involvement in Iraq: activities designed to destabilize Iraq's fragile government as the U.S. begins the process of military disengagement. A subservient Iraq has long been a goal of Iran's clerical oligarchy and of its civilian sycophants – read President Ahmadinejad. Given the already volatile and shaky nature of the "new" Iraq, the removal of U.S. troops will provide greatly increased opportunities to intervene in Iraq in order to destroy that country's nascent democratic political system and bring large parts of the country under de facto Iranian control.*

We believe that Shia forces in the country, long supported by Iran, are now receiving greatly increased Iranian assistance - covert as long as the Americans are in-country, overt once the Americans have departed.

I believe we are now seeing the first results of increased Iranian covert support for Iraq's Shia militias, and the beginning of the "final" competition between Shia and Sunni elements for dominance. In order for the Shia to begin their effort to emerge as the dominant force in the country, it is necessary for the Iraqi leadership (read: President Maliki) to remove American forces from the playing field as much as possible.

Summary Judgment: We are seeing, for the U.S., the beginning of the end: for the Iraqis, the end of the beginning of the fight to "rearrange" Iraq. Iran's essentially limitless ability to support Iraqi Shia's – and not quite to incidentally work against U.S. interests, can only serve to defeat any chance for a harmonized, democratic Iraq to exist after America departs.

Saturday, August 1, 2009

The Third Afghan War - Failed Strategies

Comment: The author worked with the Government of Pakistan while a major insurgency against the Soviet Army occupation of Afghanistan was established and brought to maturity.

"The war in Afghanistan was the last nail in the coffin of the Soviet Union"

Eduard Shevardnadze, Minister of Foreign Affairs, (last) Government of the U.S.SR

Focus

This article, the first of several on the war in Afghanistan, focuses on the USSR's strategy in its 1979 invasion of Afghanistan – which we term the "First Afghan War"; then looks at the 2001 invasion of that country by the U.S. – the "Second Afghan War"; and then considers the recent decision by the new U.S. Administration to vastly increase our troop strength in Afghanistan: an action which I call the "Third Afghan War".

The parallels between the Soviet Union's experience in nine years of war following their 1979 invasion of Afghanistan, and the consequences of America's eight years of fighting in that country after our 2001 invasion, are remarkable and ominous.

Neither country, after almost the same amount of time, was able to accomplish its strategic objectives, nor in fact, must both invasions be regarded as failures. President Obama's recent decision to very significantly increase both our military presence and economic assistance is, based on our careful study, virtually certain to fail as well.

Background

The Soviets invaded in 1979 to shore up a vassal Communist regime (with its own Soviet-supplied army and air force) which, like all its predecessor regimes over many previous centuries, was unable to control and dominate the country. The Soviets adopted a strategy that called for removing and replacing the "failed" Afghan Communist leadership (which they had previously installed in a Moscow–directed coup that expelled the Afghan royal family) plus invading and flooding the country with Soviet combat forces that were to establish and maintain a successful communist government in Kabul and the countryside.

The main enemies the U.S.SR (and its new puppet government and military) faced were the many regional tribal warlords, primarily from the Pushtoon/Pathan majority of the population, which had historically (and successfully) resisted every central government that ever claimed to run the country from Kabul. These same tribals for a thousand years had fought between themselves and against every foreign invader who came their way. In addition, the Soviets faced some limited resistance from small, poorly supplied and disorganized groups of anti-regime and anti-Soviet fighters who had spontaneously risen against the first Communist government – which they regarded as being subject to a foreign power – in this case, the USSR.

The counter to this "First Afghan War" was a U.S./Pakistani supported insurgency, which ultimately forced the Soviet withdrawal.

In the interval between the Soviet departure in 1988-1989 and U.S. invasion of 2001, Afghanistan was utterly abandoned by the Clinton Administration, which took office immediately after the Soviets withdrew. In addition to simply ignoring Afghanistan, the Clinton Administration promptly also named Pakistan a pariah, and cut-off all aid and assistance, thereby losing any possible leverage with Pakistan over post-Soviet developments in war-torn and utterly destabilized Afghanistan. This was direct "punishment" for Pakistan's on-going program to develop nuclear weapons. That program was well covered by U.S. intelligence in the Soviet-Afghan war years, but, allied with Congress, the Reagan Administration accepted the nuclear program as the price to be paid for indispensable Pakistani support for America's proxy war with the Soviets. To fill the vacuum left by the Soviet withdrawal the vicious ultra-radical Islamic Taliban (supported in part by Pakistan) fought less radical insurgent groups and took control of the country, and for over ten years terrorized domestic opposition. The Taliban also welcomed al-Qaeda, which used the country as a safe-haven and training base.

U.S. President George Bush started the "Second Afghan War" – the U.S. invasion of Afghanistan - in the immediate aftermath of the events of 9/11/2001, well before the U.S. invasion of Iraq. His rationale, accepted by America's NATO allies, was that the al-Qaeda terrorist organization (responsible for the attacks in New York) was overtly operating in, and drawing support from, the radical Islamic Taliban regime in Afghanistan. In effect, Afghanistan was seen as the principal safe haven and operations base for al-Qaeda's world-wide attacks on both western and moderate Muslim targets.

America's strategic assumption was that denying Afghanistan to both the Taliban and al-Qaeda was an absolute imperative in the war against the terrorists. This was to be accomplished by invading the country to destroy the Taliban government, and, by occupying the country and defeating any other "anti-democratic" elements, establishing a "democratic" (versus a communist) government. The latter effort was to be supported by the provision of extensive "nation building" and economic assistance, involving both NATO governments and various NGO's.

Both the U.S. and the USSR had identical goals: the establishment of viable central governments: one communist, the other democratic. And both made incorrect -and identical - strategic decisions when they launched their respective invasions. Each assumed that an effective national government of its own design could be imposed on Afghanistan - when no real government had ever existed in the country. Both utterly failed to recognize the depth of Afghan hatred of foreign invaders, and the willingness of many traditionally war-like Afghans to fight endlessly to repel them. Finally, neither country believed that its highly sophisticated and mobile armies could be defeated by "rag heads" armed only with small arms.

More than eight years of Soviet military activity in the country utterly failed to defeat the Mujahadin. That, plus the high cost of significant personnel and equipment losses, finally persuaded the Soviet Union that the war was not worth the price, and, swallowing their pride, the Soviets unilaterally withdrew from Afghanistan.

According to the best Russian sources I have been able to find, the following are key statistics:

➢ Between December 1979 and February 1989 about 620,000 Soviet military personnel served in Afghanistan: 525,000 from the Army, and 95,000 KGB border troops. In addition, about 22,000 "civilian experts" were assigned to the country.

➢ Approximately 15,000 Soviets were killed in the nine years of war, and 22,000 Soviet soldiers were wounded or disabled to the extent that they were discharged from the Army/KGB.

➢ In the same period the entire Soviet-supported Afghan Army, perhaps around 300,000 men at the start of the war, simply disintegrated. Many were killed by the Mujahadin; many defected and joined the insurgents; and the rest simply took off their uniforms and went home.

➢ It is impossible to accurately estimate Mujahadin losses in the Soviet conflict; my educated guess is that about 50,000 insurgents were killed or died of wounds in that period. An unknown – but significant – number of insurgents were then killed in vicious fighting between Taliban and non-Taliban elements as the former struggled to seize control of the country.

➢ Between five (5) to seven (7) million Afghans fled their country for refugee camps in Pakistan, largely to avoid Soviet attacks on the rural population: a Soviet tactic widely used to "deny support" to the Mujahadin.

In the 1980-1984 time period it is estimated that the Soviets maintained about 140,000 troops in-country. That troop ceiling was imposed by the Kremlin, which rejected frequent requests by Soviet 40th Army Hqs in Kabul to increase the number of troops.

Post-war comments by former senior Red Army officers suggest that Army Hqs in Kabul believed that at least 250,000 troops were needed to accomplish the Army's mission.

My own 1984 estimates (repeat estimates) of the numbers of Mujahadin involved in the insurgency were as follows: approximately 450,000 persons were armed, and considered themselves to be Mujahadin. Perhaps 100,000 of these entered Afghanistan on operations two or three times in the course of a year. At any one time,

I estimated that perhaps 15,000 – 20,000 were on the ground and actively seeking combat with the Soviets.

2001 – The Second Afghan War

With the assistance of its NATO allies (particularly the British, who, unlike in Iraq, have provided significant combat forces and actively engaged the enemy) the U.S. military was able quickly to destroy what passed for a Taliban government and semi-organized Taliban forces. In the eight years since the U.S. invasion, however, we have failed to eradicate al-Qaeda, either in Afghanistan or in Pakistan, or to defeat a wider insurgency that sprang up after the Taliban defeat. The Taliban has clearly recovered from the shock of the U.S. invasion, and has established an effective country-wide insurgency. Taliban supporters are not the only insurgents we face: plenty of "independent" groups, primarily based on their tribal affiliations, fight against the U.S. as well. Despite the deaths (as of the end of July 2009) of almost 700 U.S. soldiers, and large sums spent on military and economic support for the wildly corrupt puppet pro-American Afghan Government, it is widely agreed that the military and political situation in Afghanistan significantly deteriorated in 2008 and the first half of 2009.

The U.S. invasion of Afghanistan had the unintended consequence of, in effect, exporting the Taliban and al-Qaeda to Pakistan, with the result that Pakistan's very existence is now gravely threatened. Its survival is even more questionable the longer we are in Afghanistan. Many Taliban fighters, who are fundamentally anything but an army, fled into Pakistan's North West Frontier Province (NWFP), which the Pakistan Government has never fully controlled. Many others found sanctuary in Baluchistan, where they quite openly operate with little or no effective opposition from Pakistani Army, paramilitary or police units.

Initially limited in their ability to fight the Americans in Afghanistan, the Taliban has used its Pakistani sanctuaries to re-group in order to continue the battle in their homeland, and has found itself powerful enough to destabilize Pakistan itself.

Despite tremendous American political pressure to attack both Taliban and al-Qaeda forces – most of which were located in the tribal frontier areas with Afghanistan - the Pakistanis were reluctant to carry out extensive military operations against them. The NWFP – as under British rule – is a largely autonomous region, which the Pakistan Army stayed away from: the Pakistanis simply did not want to stir up a hornets' nest. The Pakistanis gradually agreed to step up their pressure, and are increasingly cooperating with Americans operating directly across the "formal" border with Afghanistan. They also tacitly agreed to unmanned aircraft strikes at Taliban/al-Qaeda targets in the frontier.

In part as a reaction to this surge of operations against them, and in part because their strength in manpower and arms has radically increased, Taliban elements in the NWFP actually invaded and took control of previously peaceable and more settled parts of the Province, such as the Swat District. This has shattered the Pakistan Government's hope for some sort of truce with the Taliban, and the Pakistan Army has been forced to mount major operations to recover these areas. (While claiming success in Swat, and having urged hundreds of thousands of the two million refugees from the area to return home, there are indications that the Taliban is returning to Swat, which has been left in ruins by the fighting with the Pakistan Army. It is far from clear that the government has actually won back territory temporarily seized (and brutally governed) by the Taliban.)

Thus the Pakistan Army and Government, always uneasy over U.S. pressure to attack Taliban/al-Qaeda elements in their safe havens along the frontier inside Pakistan, are, as they often warned that they might be, now confronted with open warfare inside Pakistan, against Taliban forces. The U.S. decision to greatly increase its military presence in Afghanistan, will, in the view of many Pakistanis, only serve to increase Taliban operations in Pakistan. The Pakistanis are now quietly protesting that the greatly enhanced U.S. campaign in Afghanistan will result in vastly greater Taliban challenges to them – perhaps to the point of destabilizing their already politically and economically shaky country.

These fears are well founded, and the Taliban, in part because of greater U.S. pressure in their country, will indeed grow as a threat to Pakistan. One near-term result of such increased Taliban pressure might be another Pakistan Army coup. Quite aside from again halting Pakistan's bumbling steps toward democracy, I suspect that the Army would, citing its primary mission of defending the country, shut down or radically reduce its cooperation with the U.S., thus denying the U.S. the assistance of an absolutely necessary ally.

Quite aside from the potential for losing active Pakistani military and intelligence assistance and cooperation, we must remember that the major U.S. supply line to land-locked Afghanistan is across Pakistan. Not only through the country, but directly through the frontier tribal areas now either tacitly or actually controlled by the Taliban. It would be impossible to sustain U.S. forces in Afghanistan if Pakistan either revokes permission for U.S. to transit the country – or tacitly allows the Taliban to "close the passes" in the mountainous frontier to the U.S.

My key point here is that the U.S. must consider which goal is most important: a) creating a vaguely stable "friendly" country by fighting a major counter-insurgency in Afghanistan for as long as ten years (a time frame recently posited by Defense Secretary Bob Gates); or b) helping a nuclear-armed Pakistan survive the grave challenges currently posed by an active and growing Taliban - assisted by plenty of home-grown and well-armed Islamic radicals. Like it or not, these are not complementary objectives.

The 2009 "Third Afghan War" Decision

The President's early 2009 decision to more than double U.S. troop strength in Afghanistan – made as a result of increased insurgent activities and success and larger U.S. casualties - should be regarded as much more than "just" a continuation of "President Bush's" 2001 invasion.

While his decision could be seen as a re-affirmation of the earlier Bush/Soviet strategies, the very large force increase and much advertised changes in the tactical deployment of our troops represent the start of a totally new war, which I have labeled the "Third Afghan War".

Careful examinations of all of the factors that have heretofore denied both the Soviets and us success in Afghanistan are persuasive arguments against the Third War.

The U.S. Invasion - Analysis

I believe that America's strategic decision in 2001 that a full-scale invasion was a necessary part of the U.S. effort to deal with al-Qaeda was totally flawed. Further, the concurrent decision to occupy Afghanistan to establish and by force defend a new government obviously did not take into account the very real possibility of a protracted and costly counter insurgency effort.

At no time did the Taliban itself threaten or attack the U.S. In fact, the last thing that the Taliban wanted was war with the U.S. While ideologically in tune with al-Qaeda, the latter was essentially a "guest" in Afghanistan. The Taliban, however distasteful it was to most foreigners, was NOT a threat to the United States, and was NOT seeking a fight with America.

True, permission to operate and the provision of safe havens for training and organization in Afghanistan was given by the Taliban, but al-Qaeda operated in a very limited number of locations, and was not supported or defended by the Taliban. A much more surgical approach would almost certainly have been able to destroy most al-Qaeda elements in the country. Given America's extensive Special Forces assets; intelligence capabilities (signals and satellite, if nothing else); its aviation and infantry night fighting capabilities, plus having assured staging and recovery areas in Pakistan, it is surprising that the Americans made the error of choosing to mount a full-scale invasion. Such strikes would, no doubt, have had to be repeated, and probably would not have done any more or less damage to al-Qaeda. But they would have been vastly cheaper in terms of blood and money. Also, surgical strikes from Pakistan would not have driven both the Taliban and al-Qaeda into Pakistan, a consequence which has had such disastrous results for that country.

Assuming that the U.S. did not in 2001 envisage an open-ended, i.e., unlimited, presence in Afghanistan, the 2001 decision to invade was followed by what we see as an even more illogical decision to remain in the country and "re-build" it after "destroying" the Taliban militarily. In making that strategic policy decision the U.S. clearly did not give sufficient thought to the possibility of being faced with a major guerrilla war – which we should have assumed was at least a strong possibility given the Soviet experience following their 1979 invasion. One would also think that the U.S. would have carefully considered the character of who it would be fighting in Afghanistan; the nature of the terrain, etc.: realities which were exposed by the Soviet Union from 1979 until the Soviet withdrawal in 1989.

I have emphasized the adverse consequences of the Second Afghan War's "invade and stay" strategy because (irrespective of President Obama's recent decision to increase our force levels) this is a moment in time where we can and should challenge the continuation of a strategy/policy that has failed U.S. for the past eight years; failed the Soviet Union before us; and, I think, will fail us now.

I am not alone in suggesting that remaining in Afghanistan will be a near-term (1 to 3 years) failure, or just possibly a long-term (up to 10 years) success. Our NATO allies unanimously rejected Mr. Obama's early 2009 request for additional NATO military forces in Afghanistan. NATO clearly signaled that it does not believe that the stay/fight/develop strategy will work, or at least not work in a time period that they and their voters will politically accept. Even Britain, which has the second largest number of combat forces in the country, is increasingly uncomfortable about the open-ended aspect of the war.

Note: The NATO reaction to President Obama's request for force increases was not, apparently, given much importance by the Administration or Congress. This is a major error, since it should serve as an important vote against the Administration's new open-ended commitments in Afghanistan.

Immediate Threats and Problems

There are at least 4 key factors that must be addressed immediately, and factored into the "Third War" decision.

Iran's recent internal turmoil, which is far from resolved, has caused a dramatic up-tick in anti-U.S. sentiments on the part of President Ahmadinejad and his supporters – particularly in the Revolutionary Guard. This animosity will be amplified by the U.S. pressure on Iran over the nuclear issue.

I expect that Iran will view the Third Afghan War as an inexpensive, plausibly deniable, and easy-to-execute opportunity to "pay back" and damage the U.S. I expect to see vastly increased support for the insurgents by Iran's Revolutionary Guard. The long border with Afghanistan makes it easy for the insurgents to cross to Iranian safe-havens to receive arms, funds and training from the Iranians. In effect, Iran will become to the U.S. what Pakistan was to the Soviets. If this happens, the adverse consequences to the Americans would be severe. At the very least increased Iranian support would drive up U.S. casualties and prolong the War for as long as there are significant numbers of insurgents left alive to fight. The Revolutionary Guard is a virtually inexhaustible source of well armed and trained "volunteers" to bolster the insurgents.

The threat to Pakistan's continued existence as a nuclear-armed but non-radical Islamic country will increase in direct ratio to a) the length of time U.S. troops are in Afghanistan, and b) to the aggressiveness of both our forces and the insurgents. Pakistan already sees this connection, and, we believe, will become an increasingly reluctant ally. If we are so blind as to ignore the possibility of Pakistan's cutting our irreplaceable supply routes we are building our war on sand.

If the Pakistanis do continue to provide their indispensable support for our greatly expanded war, we must consider the likely consequences to their internal stability, and be prepared to provide very large additional amounts of aid to help them counter and defeat domestic radical Islamic elements. Those elements have wide support, and have often proven that they are more than willing to resort to violence against both civilian and Pakistani military targets. I believe that these domestic extremist Islamic groups already have sufficient strength to virtually shut-down the country. They have long been fertile recruiting grounds for both the Taliban and al-Qaeda, and their association with radical elements from Afghanistan could eventually result in the creation of a nuclear-armed radical Islamic country. We must look beyond Afghanistan as we consider the consequences of a Third Afghan War.

Questions

If one looks at the Administration's present course of action, and its intentions regarding Afghanistan, the following questions come immediately to mind.

First, what are the President's objectives in a Third Afghan War, and are they sufficiently valid to merit up to a decade of U.S. sacrifice in both blood and money?

I believe not. What would it really mean to us if Afghanistan returns to crazed Taliban rule, or to its centuries-old tradition of endless internal strife? We don't live there, and we are not somehow morally obliged to try to "protect the Afghan people", and/or to create a "modern" and "democratic" government and state. If we were, we should also be fighting in half a dozen countries around the world. Need we, for example, invade and "sort out" Sudan? Should we intervene militarily in Saudi Arabia to champion women's rights and unseat the corrupt Saudi monarchy? Afghanistan has no strategic or economic value to us – none.

It is postulated by the Administration that we must remain to fight – apparently endlessly – in Afghanistan in order to defeat al-Qaeda, and, presumably to prevent other al-Qaeda type groups from using the country as a refuge. This is nonsense: al-Qaeda lives, as do many other terrorist groups. By staging our trained and highly-capable forces in Pakistan we could, given decent intelligence, strike terrorists in Afghanistan whenever and wherever we wished – and then withdraw. We do not need a huge physical presence in the country to attack high-value terrorist targets (i.e., terrorists who are a threat to the U.S.).

With the lessons of two previous failed Afghan wars before him, why is the President determined to repeat the same failed strategy? How many times must a game plan fail before it is abandoned? Having won election in part because of his opposition to the Iraq War, what accounts for his decision not only to remain in Afghanistan but to radically expand the war? Viewed through an intelligence assessment lens, the inescapable question arises: is that decision basically a political move intended to show that he is "tough on terrorism"? Or is he so confident of his personal assessment of the situation that he is, in effect, relying on his intuition?

Wars need public and Congressional support and funding. A Congress dominated by the Democratic Party (and Mr. Obama himself) bitterly opposed President Bush's Iraq policy – as did the American left wing. But so far, neither the Congress nor the left have spoken against his expansion plans. Why? Does Mr. Obama believe that his personal magnetism is so great that he can safely assume that Congress and the electorate will accept what is now "his war" – another interminable, costly, and probably unwinnable struggle that will drag on for many years? Or will Congress (and the country) tolerate a few years of war and then pull the plug?

A basic premise in Mr. Obama's Third War strategy is that U.S. troops can quickly train Afghan military and police units, and have them do the fighting – reducing U.S. troop strength as the Afghans increasingly take up the burden. This concept is what U.S. commanders now place their hopes and plans on.

> ➤ This is exactly the strategy we have used in Iraq, and, given Mr. Obama's time-table for withdrawal from that country, the premise is now being tested there. Few dispassionate observers think it will succeed. Even fewer qualified foreign observers believe it can work in Afghanistan.

> ➤ It is, in theory, a valid one, and a classic formulation for fighting a counter-insurgency war.

> ➤ It was tried in Vietnam, and it failed.

> ➤ It was tried by the Soviets, who "inherited" a large communist army in Afghanistan, and it failed.

> ➤ It has been underway in Afghanistan for years, and, to this point, it has utterly failed.

I believe that every indicator strongly argues that it will fail in a Third Afghan War unless the U.S. is prepared to maintain much larger forces than are now envisaged, as well as an enormous and expanded economic assistance program for a decade or more. Why?

> ➤ No living Afghan believes the U.S. will stay the course – Iraq proves their point. Further, as in Iraq, the bottom line for every Afghan is to be on the winning side after the Americans leave – which they surely will. In my opinion most Afghans believe that the "winning side" will not be the side the Americans support. So an army and police structure can be built slowly, but it will fragment and return to its traditional loyalties once America departs.

> ➤ We are most emphatically not dealing with an Afghan population that is prepared to fight for the ideals of democracy. Absent a country-wide commitment to "democratic" economic and political goals, which we will not see in several lifetimes, Afghans ultimately will give their allegiance to their traditional tribal/regional affiliations: not to a government in Kabul.

Is Pakistan more important to U.S. than Afghanistan? I would emphatically say yes.

A Final Thought

> ➤ Our actions to suppress/destroy the vast opium poppy fields in Afghanistan will alienate a huge percentage of the very population we must depend on for assistance – or at least neutrality – in a counter-insurgency.

> ➤ No one, anywhere, has yet devised a means to entice poppy producers to grow more benign crops. There are no economically viable (and therefore acceptable to poppy growers) alternate crops. Nor can we allow poppy growth and then buy (and destroy) the product ourselves to keep it off the world market. To make such an offer would result in poppies

being grown on every square inch of arable land in the country. And we would have to beat whatever prices the drug dealers are willing to "bid" against us.

Conclusion

My analysis of the Afghan wars has led me to object strongly to the President's policy. I do not believe that we should be fighting a Third Afghan War.

That said, the grim reality is that the country – including, apparently, the anti-Iraq War left wing and Congress – will tolerate many American lives lost, billions wasted, and Pakistan – at a minimum – increasingly unhappy and destabilized. Why the liberal/left wing has not objected to - or at least challenged - the Third Afghan War is beyond my understanding – as is the fact that the Republican minority in Congress raises no questions on the wisdom of fighting the new war. Are we sheep being led to the slaughter?

Saturday, August 22, 2009

Comment by Former Secretary of State, Lawrence Eagleburger on Failed Strategies

These comments were made by former Secretary of State Lawrence Eagleburger on my article, "The Third Afghan War – Failed Strategies" of 1 August 2009.

I have seen your most recent article on Afghanistan. Congratulations, it is superb! As you know, I had been thinking about doing something myself, to follow up on the piece I had done some months ago, but, as I told you, I have identified another subject on which I intend to focus. Further, you have covered all the points I would have made – and more eloquently and nuanced than I would have done. I hope you are going to follow-up with another article.

Let me very briefly summarize my concerns. We are already repeating some of the actions that give me an uncomfortable "Vietnam" feeling:

a) Deploying insufficient numbers of troops to accomplish the mission (defeat the insurgents;

b) Deploying (dribbling in) additional troops in order to "win" without ever defining what we consider winning to be;

c) Indigenous forces that are not up to our standards thereby forcing U.S. to put in more forces to "train" them;

d) Plus one very significant additional factor – the tenuous condition of our "ally". Pakistan is in delicate shape and I suspect that our presence contributes more than a little bit to its instability.

And finally, I am less than enthusiastic about having to depend on the Paks for our resupply lifeline.

You will, I know, cover all this and more in anything you do. I fear that we will repeat another mistake we made in Vietnam and fail to listen to critics, but as often in the life of governments, it is ever so even when that government has people who have been all through this before.

Tuesday, August 25, 2009

The Third Afghan War - Part Two

Introduction

In a 1 August 2009 article titled "The Third Afghan War – Failed Strategies" I wrote that from a purely intelligence perspective the war in Afghanistan, specifically President Obama's recent decision to greatly increase our presence and role in that country (which I have termed the Third Afghan War), is an enormous mistake that will result in a costly failure.

This is a follow-on article. I begin with my conclusions and a plea that the President's decision be challenged and reversed. I then provide commentary that supports those conclusions by providing more information on key aspects of the Afghan situation.

My analysis is not an "armchair" exercise: for over three years in the early 1980's my job was to establish and bring to maturity a successful anti-Soviet insurgency in Afghanistan; an insurgency that eventually caused the Soviet Union to withdraw from that country. I spent many hundreds of hours working directly with the Afghan Mujahadin (Freedom Fighters) and our Pakistan Army colleagues to devise strategies and tactics appropriate to the Afghan battlefield. This essentially meant learning as much as possible about the country, customs, psychology and attitudes of the people doing the actual fighting; and tailoring weapons, tactics and training to match these realities.

Conclusions

President Obama's – and NATO's – primary justification for the continuation of the war in Afghanistan is that the Taliban must be destroyed, and Afghanistan made into some sort of stable state, in order to deny al-Qaeda a safe-haven from which to attack the United States (and Europe).

Similar reasoning, advanced during the Bush presidency, resulted in our invading the country in 2001: a decision that has led to eight years of inconclusive and costly war against Taliban and other insurgents. Observers now agree that the situation has greatly worsened over the past several years: NATO troop losses are significantly higher, and the insurgents are fighting with increasing sophistication and success. The new commander of U.S. and NATO forces in Afghanistan, General Stanley McChrystal, stated earlier this month that the Taliban have gained the upper hand in the war.

Faced by this negative state of affairs, the President has asserted that the defeat of al-Qaeda depends on our continuing to occupy and wage war in Afghanistan; and that to do that the U.S. must now significantly increase our force levels and economic assistance, and prepare for a "long war"- lasting perhaps ten years. Further, "nation building" now appears to be the President's primary intention. In effect, he seeks to apply the old Vietnam formula – send more troops and spend more money.

This is an incorrect assessment with long-term fatal consequences.

Al-Qaeda has long since fled to Pakistan, where it is now firmly ensconced. Al-Qaeda should be fought in Pakistan, not in Afghanistan, where we are actually fighting the Taliban and other insurgents. IF we were to abandon Afghanistan and small units of al-Qaeda were to return, they could easily be attacked by raids by U.S. Special Forces troops based in Pakistan. We do not need to fight a major war against a completely unrelated enemy – the Taliban and other insurgent groups – in order to fight and defeat al-Qaeda. Further, it is logical to assume that al-Qaeda, if it were forced to abandon its Pakistani sanctuaries, would move to another country – Somalia, for example.

Leaving Afghanistan would enable us to shift resources to help protect a nuclear-armed country that for many reasons deserves our assistance, and where, unlike Afghanistan, a government and a competent (anti-radical Islamic) Army exist. Finally, the war in Afghanistan has greatly increased militant Islamic (including insurgent) activity in Pakistan, with the result that that already unstable country is under unprecedented internal stress. Pakistan, I submit, for many reasons would welcome our withdrawal from Afghanistan, and permit us to establish low visibility bases from which our troops could, if necessary, launch raids against any al-Qaeda elements that might surface in Afghanistan. *NOTE: It is important to remember that not all radical/militant Muslims are insurgents. Further, not all insurgents in Afghanistan or Pakistan are Taliban.*

The President has responded to the deteriorating situation in Afghanistan by ordering a significant increase of troop strength, and a complete change in our strategy of fighting the war. Rather than having American combat forces seek out, engage and destroy insurgent elements - a strategy which has largely failed - they are now to be spread across the entire country to "protect the people." Thus assuming a basically defensive posture while we increase our "nation building" activities. At the same time field commanders have been instructed, in order to reduce "collateral damage" (i.e., the deaths of innocent civilians) to limit the use of the air and artillery strikes that have long provided our troops a major combat advantage and reduced our own casualties. Finally, while our troop strength has been roughly doubled to about 60,000 men, no one believes that number is adequate to the task. I have seen reports that field commanders have been all but ordered NOT to ask for still more troops. I believe, however, that more troops will be asked for, and that we will eventually field a total of about 80,000 U.S. troops.

Given the realities of Afghan society, and the nature of the insurgents we are fighting, I believe that President Obama's new strategy is a guaranteed recipe for failure, and is, in fact, self-defeating. While in theory we will lose fewer troops by abandoning aggressive search-and-kill missions, we will be setting up targets across the country that are perfectly suited to the insurgent's attack capabilities. It is certain that there will not be enough troops, and that they will be spread too thinly. These dispositions will actually invite insurgent attack, since the enemy can now muster fighters and firepower to attack carefully selected and lightly garrisoned American outposts at the time and place of their choosing, and will have excellent intelligence to assist them in these attacks.

What to Do?

We - the American people, the Congress, our senior military and the members of the Administration's foreign policy team - are now, after eight plus years of indecisive and costly fighting in Afghanistan, at a decision point. We can either dutifully accept the President's policy, OR work to prompt a review which, by presenting factual evidence based on eight years of fighting and recent developments in the country, might lead him to change his mind.

If he does not, then Congress, which controls the money, must act to end the "Third Afghan War" - now. NOT after an "as yet undetermined" additional number of Americans are killed, and billions more dollars that we do not have are spent. Democrats who so opposed the Iraq War, but who thus far have gone along with the President, must have the guts to vote against their party's President and their party leadership. Republicans must end their knee-jerk support for the War.

If our Department of Defense leadership, our intelligence agency chiefs, and our State Department and National Security Council leadership do NOT in their souls believe that we should be fighting this fight, but believe that it is most likely that we will eventually walk away from Afghanistan having failed, they must stand up and say so.

I truly understand and once served my country under the precept that those of us who do (or did) serve the President should be "loyal" and support his policies. There is, however, a greater obligation – to the best interests of our country and to the citizens we serve. Presidents can be wrong: as Lyndon Johnson was in Vietnam. This is far too great an issue - we are dealing with ordering the deaths and dreadful wounding of our soldiers, and the destruction of their families - to simply submit to the "I am loyal to my President and am just following orders" school of behavior. Ask the men who brought us the Vietnam War, and lived in painful remorse ever after.

There is a way for our civilian leadership to honorably disagree with a President: make a thoughtful statement of why, and resign. No one at senior levels of the Administration depends on their government salaries. Nor, and this is perhaps most important, should the natural inclination to remain in positions of power justify not taking a principled stand when the issue is as grave as fighting a wrong - and almost certainly un-winnable war.

The above is a carefully considered plea to those holding High Office in this land to study the Afghan "problem" in its entirety and, if intelligence and instinct clearly indicate that we should NOT begin this Third Afghan War, to say so, and to do something about it.

It is also a plea to anyone who has been gracious enough to read this, and agrees with my basic conclusions, to contact those in High Office and ask that they act to prevent this country from enduring what will become another Vietnam.

The Afghan Insurgent

The following is an attempt to provide some insight into why, how, and for what the Afghan insurgent fights, and a quick review of other issues that are crucial to our ability to win in Afghanistan.

The societal and philosophical mindset of any enemy is always an important consideration: this is of particularly vital importance in the Afghan War. The closest parallel to the Afghan insurgent is, I think, the World War II Japanese soldier, whose societal and psychological underpinning made him the fearsome, tough and unyielding warrior he was. Equally important are the more general economic and social realities of the country.

Most Afghan insurgents - and I wish to stress again that not all insurgents are "Taliban" – are "tribals" from the mountainous Pushtun and Tajik areas of the country. Over half of the population of Afghanistan is comprised of Pushtuns (about 43 percent) and Tajiks (about 22 percent). For over two thousand years of history, most importantly from the 1700's to the present, the tribes of Afghanistan have repeatedly shown that they are perhaps the most independent, martial, bellicose and xenophobic peoples in the world. The Pushtuns fought the British Indian Empire to a standstill in the 19th century: on one occasion literally annihilating an entire British Indian Army which invaded Afghanistan – from which disaster exactly one man returned to British India alive. In my opinion the Pushtuns, Tajiks and their ilk are the bravest, most resilient and determined guerilla fighters in the world. Every Pushtun considers himself a warrior, which he has been bred to be. He loves to fight, expects and gives no quarter, and considers death in combat a reward. Any opponent who does not recognize the indomitable spirit, physical hardiness and general mental framework of these tribal fighters – as the Soviets failed to do – is destined to pay a heavy price.

It is almost impossible to properly explain the proclivity that these people, particularly the Pushtuns, have for fighting. No male Pushtun, since firearms were introduced to the area in the early 1700's, considers himself a man until he has armed himself with a rifle. Further, no Pushtun is a man until he has used that rifle: whether against a rival tribe, "the government", or a foreign presence. The process of becoming a warrior begins as soon as a male child can walk: the long days and nights of his youth are spent listening to tales, many of them true, of the valor and spirit of his elders fighting against "the enemy." These rugged, ragged, desperately poor and virile mountain people have constructed a society where martial valor is the ultimate badge of manhood and a total way of life. These are not mere words: there is no equivalent society anywhere else in the world. They are Spartans without a Sparta.

Mobility

The traditional Afghan mode of fighting was and is to form a lashgar – an armed band that goes forth to attack an enemy and then retreats to its own safe area after the action. We found in the First Afghan War (that against the Soviets) that we could convert the concept of the lashgar into what in modern military parlance is called a strike team or a strike force. This could range in size from 20 to 200 men. Operating from a safe haven, usually in Pakistan or in an area of Afghanistan where no enemy troops were present, the lashgar would identify a specific target, calculate the number of days it would take to move to and remain in the target area, and select the weapons that it would need. For example, whether in addition to small arms it would it require a heavy load of RPGs, mortar shells, or explosives. Generally speaking, the lashgar would carry with it all of the food, ammunition, and weapons each person required for the mission: no provision was made to provide transportation or resupply. *NOTE: It was very often possible for a lashgar to use vehicles to drive a fair distance towards their target area, then dismount and complete the journey on foot - a practice intended to evade enemy reconnaissance aircraft. While Soviet air reconnaissance capabilities pale in comparison to that available to U.S. forces, I am told by Pakistani sources that this procedure is still utilized.*

The ability of the insurgents to carry all their weapons and food is remarkable. An insurgent needs and carries only his rifle, ammunition, an RPG or other additional weapon, water, salt, tea, chapattis (tortillas), and sugar. He wears his ordinary clothing (by choice, since it enables him to drop his weapons load and pass for "just another Afghan"). He expects no resupply in the course of his mission. He will, if he is lucky, obtain a few hot meals from sedentary farmers, but once a lashgar sets out on a mission it expects and generally receives no support along the way. Compare this to an American unit, where each soldier carries a 70 to 90 pound pack on his back, plus his weapons. That unit requires frequent resupply by air if it is to be away from its base for more than a few days. *COMMENT: In the First Afghan War the insurgents also carried into and around Afghanistan large numbers of heavy crew-served weapons, primarily 12.7 and 14.5 machine guns for use against aircraft. Given American reconnaissance capabilities they now seldom make any attempt to lug these kinds of weapons around. Today's insurgent is well aware of U.S. day and night reconnaissance activity, and responds by using smaller lashgars, split up for the walking phase, and often moves during daylight hours when a handful of individuals may attract less attention.*

Loyalties

An Afghan's loyalties lie totally with his tribe and sub-tribe. The importance of this tribal loyalty to each individual cannot be overstated: there is no equivalent in any Western society. Such loyalty is permanent, cannot be abandoned, and is not transferable. Punishment for violating this code is usually a brutal death, mandated by tribal elders meeting in council (a "jirga"). A father must, and will, execute his own son if the tribal jirga so mandates. Tribal loyalty is the glue that holds Pushtun society together. This has always meant that such rudimentary governance as has ever existed in the country has been the result of various tribes associating with regional tribal "super chiefs" (the "war lords" so often mentioned in the press). And no regional "super chief", no matter how well he is bribed or effusive in his assertions of loyalty, will ever truly subordinate himself to some higher (i.e., national) authority.

The strength of this tribal loyalty has many consequences: for example, it is very difficult to amalgamate groups from different tribes, many of which have a long history of inter-tribal fighting. This obstructs efforts to create organizations of such size (e.g., an Army) that must "mix" tribal units. Further, Afghans serving with central or regional government organizations – police, military, or civil – are always subject to the pull of their primary loyalty to the tribe. This means, for example, that units of the growing Afghan army and police are inherently susceptible to demands placed on them to be loyal to the tribe rather than the army. There is no repeat no concept in a tribal's mind of a regional, much less national, government: there is no government, nor should there be. Finally, the concept of being loyal to a foreign (or foreign-sponsored) government or military organization is repugnant: one may be sure that if an individual is forced to choose between tribal loyalty or loyalty to a "foreign" entity he will choose his tribe.

Another way to approach this important subject is to ask "What is an Afghan?" Or, is there a real Afghan identity? The answer is that "an Afghan" is nothing more than a person living inside a geographic area depicted on a map whose native language is not Persian, Russian, Hindustani or Urdu – the languages of neighboring states. In other words, if you live within the map boundaries and speak Pashto, Dari, Tajik or myriad other odd languages, you are an Afghan.

There is not, and never has been, anything remotely approaching a shared national identity: to say nothing of a half-way viable central – or even regional – government. Such "central government" as has ever existed in Kabul is/was largely fiction. Generally the senior warlords in the Kabul area would chose one of their own and agree, in return for a share in the spoils of a fantasy central government, to acknowledge one of their number as King-Emir-Boss. The rest of the country paid lip-service to the minimal extent possible. It has always been this way, and it is now (with the additional burden of illegitimacy, since the "government" is understood to be a creature of foreign invaders – the Americans.)

An Afghan Army

The administration is pinning its hopes on the creation of an effective Afghan Army, loyal to the government in Kabul, which will replace U.S. and NATO forces. I contend that this is a hope that cannot become a reality.

At the start of the First Afghan War (against the Soviets) there was a large Communist trained and equipped Afghan Army. These Communist troops initially – and briefly – fought against the growing insurgency. Once it became clear, however, that the insurgent forces they confronted were growing, well armed, and highly motivated the Army simply disintegrated. In effect, the soldiers would not stay loyal to the central government when they were urged by fellow tribals to either defect or just go home.

Further, a favorite insurgent tactic was to recruit fellow tribals in the Army as spies, and thus obtain complete intelligence on a regular basis. Soviet units fighting alongside Afghan Army troops quickly learned that when the going got rough their "allies" took off their uniforms and disappeared, often hooking up temporarily with the local Mujahadin to pass along any intelligence they had. Mujahadin commanders could easily pass and receive messages from Afghan army garrisons, and often instructed Afghan soldiers who otherwise wanted to desert to remain with their units to provide intelligence. Their reward was advance warning when a garrison or outpost was to be attacked.

I see little reason why this pattern will not be repeated as Afghan Army and police units are trained and expanded, and I think that creating an army and police force that is and will remain loyal to a central government is in fact impossible. Any central government is by definition regarded as threatening and hostile, and in today's Afghanistan that government, like its army and police forces, is widely regarded with contempt as creatures of the foreign invaders that support them.

I submit that the issue before the U.S. and NATO is not so much the raising and training a new Afghan Army: the problem, downstream, is whose army (or armies) are we training? My Pakistani sources tell me that many tribal chiefs/"warlords" have approved their supporters joining the "new model Army" for the express reason that it will eventually provide them (and not the central government) with the best trained and equipped soldiers in the country. In other words, they expect much of the Army to disintegrate into its tribal/regional components and return to the fold.

A final and very important consideration to raising a national army and police force: no sensible Afghan believes that U.S./NATO forces will remain in the country long enough to see a secure, effective and lasting central government established. Everyone "knows" that the foreigners will leave – probably sooner than later. The ultimate key to survival in Afghanistan (as in Iraq) – is to be on the winning side when the war is over: in this case when the Americans leave.

Honor

Outside of his immediate tribe, the average Afghan tribal is an untrustworthy, lazy, thieving, lying individual. In fact, it is a matter of considerable pride to lie, cheat, and steal – particularly when dealing with "outsiders".

An "old British Indian Army hand," an officer with decades of service on the Northwest Frontier, told me many years ago that

"Afghans are so crooked that when they die you screw them into the ground". There is much truth in that witticism. By the same token if a tribal leader gives you his promise and actually means it he and his tribe will go to the ends of the earth to honor the obligation. The problem comes in being able to tell at the outset whether he means it, and it is always best to assume that he does not.

Tactics

At the start of the First Afghan War the nascent insurgent movement relied upon ancient tactics: a gaggle of armed men would rush a target expecting to overwhelm it, disregarding expected minimal losses. They quickly discovered this was not a sensible thing to do. Their other primary tactic was the ambush, a stratagem that they developed while confronting the British Indian Army and, much later, the Soviets. A handful of tribals on top of a mountain ridge line could and did stop a British column in its tracks. The ambush and sniping were among the most successful tactics used by the Mujahadin, who quickly learned that an ambush is, in effect, a force-multiplier. By the early 1980's the Mujahadin had developed ambushing into an art form. Their success in operating with RPGs and mines against Soviet columns of both armored and soft-skinned vehicles was impressive. They were not repeat not in the least disconcerted by the Soviet's use of armored vehicles – the RPG was and is the great equalizer.

Vast quantities of small arms and ammunition were moved into the country in the First War, and it was common practice for insurgents to siphon off (from group arms dumps) quantities of weapons and ammunition for "private storage" in home villages. I doubt that there is a village in Pakistan's Frontier Province, or in Afghan territory in the South and East of the country, that does not have a reserve of weapons cleverly cached against a rainy day.

IEDs were not a major insurgent weapon in the First Afghan War: Instead they made heavy use of conventional anti-tank mines. Unlike their Iraqi counterparts, Afghan insurgents did not inherit a large supply of artillery shells to use in making IEDs. They have clearly figured out how to make do without these easily converted explosives, and in present day Afghanistan IEDs have grown to be the most effective weapon against NATO forces. The sophistication of the IEDs laid down by the insurgents has increased radically over the past several years, as has their use. Since I believe that the Iranians will substantially increase their covert support for insurgent groups in Afghanistan, one of the first and best indicators of such support will be the emergence of yet more and more sophisticated IEDs. (I also expect to see the Iranians provide stand-off weapons like mortars for use against fixed American positions.)

Although initially reluctant to attack aggressive Soviet combat units using armored vehicles, the Mujahadin, once they had sufficient quantities of land mines and RPGs, quickly became adept at attacking such units – in fact Soviet patrols, large or small, became targets of choice. Since vehicles are forced to use roads or tracks the Mujahadin could choose their ambush positions, lay mines and/or deploy RPGs which forced the attackers to halt, and then wait for infantry to dismount to engage them. From their concealed positions the Mujahadin would lay down small arms fire (usually never particularly well aimed) for a period of minutes, and then, anticipating a Soviet call for helicopter gunship support, break off the attack.

I was frequently surprised by the fact that the Mujahadin were very often able to correctly estimate the time they had to engage dismounted Soviet soldiers before the arrival of air support. On occasion it seemed almost eerie – but I suspect that their timing was based on excellent intelligence on what air assets the Soviets could call on, and the time it would take them to reach the ambush area.

Intelligence

It is an absolute given that insurgents will have very complete tactical intelligence on U.S./NATO troops, particularly on the units deployed around the country in small towns and villages. Everyone from children begging for candy bars to village elders is reporting to local insurgents. Every police or army unit operating with or near U.S. units will contain Taliban (or other insurgent) penetrations/informants. The same thing is true as one goes up the chain of command: Kabul and provincial capitals all have more than their share of informants. The recruitment of informants is a simple matter: informants either volunteer their services or, primarily in Taliban areas, are forced into the role by threats of reprisals.

Ancillary Issues

One must always remember that Afghanistan is not like Iraq: the latter is very much an urban country/society, while Afghanistan is a rural one. This means that the population is spread over a much wider area, a fact that adds greatly to the difficulty of providing "public safety". There is just too much ground to cover, which of course makes the lack of very large numbers of troops a tremendous handicap.

Large parts of the country are well suited to guerilla operations: except for flat deserts there are endless hiding places in mountains or semi-mountainous areas. There are few roads, which effectively channels vehicular traffic to a limited (and easily attacked) number of routes. Our vehicles are sitting ducks.

The long borders between the country and Iran and Pakistan are, to say the least, porous. This has made smuggling a centuries-old major business activity. Insurgents and their weapons can cross these borders with near impunity, particularly if vehicles are not used. In the first Afghan War many thousands of tons of weapons were moved from Pakistan into Afghanistan. Despite major Soviet efforts to interdict this traffic, very little was ever captured by the Soviets: weapons transport losses were, as a practical matter, nil.

After almost thirty years of continuous war the more sedentary rural Afghans, who frequently endure fighting on their very doorsteps, are fed-up. This makes many of them care less about who wins than just having the fighting end. The fact that U.S. and NATO troops are now being deployed to protect them is hardly good news. First, they too know that the Americans will "soon" leave, so that the protection is illusory, and very temporary. Second, they know perfectly well that the NATO troops living amongst them are inviting targets for insurgent attack – which will make them targets as well.

Recent orders to U.S. forces to cut back significantly on the use of artillery and air strikes are welcome news to both the people and the insurgents. These orders will, I suspect, have several negative results. First, it will probably mean that insurgents will make more tactical use of populated villages and farm houses both as assembly/rest areas and as defendable fighting points. This is the "human shield" potential. Second, it means that offensive patrols by our troops, which will now lack the immediate air/artillery support that is frequently called-in when units are attacked, will probably take significantly higher losses.

The poppy problem: U.S. and British troops have been waging several types of campaigns to limit/eradicate Afghanistan's opium production. Without going into detail, such efforts are bound to alienate poppy growers (and thus increase their support for the insurgents) and, in the end, fail. Many years of efforts in South America to accomplish the exact same end have failed, and attempting to do this while seeking to build local support in the middle of an insurgency, while a commendable goal, is questionable at the least.

Corruption has always been rampant in Afghanistan. Observers now state that it has risen to extraordinary heights. From the Afghan soldiers and police who demand petty bribes and pay-offs to really heavy corruption in Kabul and the provincial capitals, anything or anyone connected with or representing the central government is (usually correctly) believed to be on the take. This has, of course, added to the general lack of support by the public for the government, and appears to be alienating ever-larger numbers of Afghans, while providing propaganda fodder for the insurgents.

Final Comment

It would be a grand thing indeed to rid the world of Taliban and other insurgents; to eliminate al-Qaeda; to create a moderately effective and efficient government, army and police force; to establish basic democracy; to eliminate opium production; to spur economic development; to foster education and women's rights; and bring peace to Afghanistan. That is precisely the task that has been given to our troops and civilian personnel in Afghanistan.

Thursday, August 27, 2009

Comment from Former Secretary of State, Lawrence Eagleburger

Howard: I told you, when your first article on Afghanistan was published on your blog, that I thought you were on the mark in your analysis of the Administration's Afghan policy. Now that I have read your sequel I am ready to go beyond that rare compliment to an observation that is both heartfelt and painful. Heartfelt because I know how much experience, energy, and wisdom have gone into the product, and painful, both because of how clearly it demonstrates that history does indeed repeat itself, and because you and I both know that those who have set our country on this course will not retreat from it until we have paid a terrible price.

I am willing to concede that there are differences in circumstance, geography, and people between Viet Nam and Afghanistan. The similarities, however, are compelling: a body politic that is fragmented and lacking the resources and will to defend itself, motivated enemies supplied from outside, an American administration unwilling to commit at the outset whatever force might prove necessary to "win", an American populace that is ambivalent about the war and likely to become ever more negative as casualties mount, etc., etc. etc. Add to this witches brew the fact that we must rely on Pakistan for everything from supply routes to intelligence and political stability, and you will be excused for pessimism and a serious reason for questioning the Administration's course.

All of this, my friend, you have laid out with clarity and eloquence. I could wish that senior people in the Obama Administration could see your article and act upon it with wisdom. But that is the price we pay for an administration short on personnel with national and foreign affairs experience. Even when we have a Secretary of Defense with that experience it counts for naught.

Howard, you are standing in the way of actions that -- if continued -- will greatly harm the nation. You have my admiration.

Friday, September 18, 2009

Nuclear Iran: Get Used to It

Events over the past weeks have clearly indicated that Iran will not respond to either U.S. or U.N. Security Council demands that the country stop its nuclear weapons program. By the end of this month the Obama Administration will - hopefully -acknowledge that there is no point in attempting to have the President enter into unilateral discussions with Iranian President Ahmadinejad. Further, Russia and China have made crystal clear that they will not support any really serious. increase in U.N. sanctions - which they can and will veto on the odd chance proposals for stronger sanctions actually reach the Council.

Given the above realities, following is my assessment of the options available to President Obama in dealing with Iran.

1. *An expansion of sanctions by the U.S. - either alone or in conjunction with whatever (inevitably very mild) additional sanctions the EU might be willing to impose.*

Assessment: A limited increase in sanctions would only slightly add to the inconveniences Iran now faces from existing sanctions, and would not under any circumstances force Iran to terminate its nuclear weapons program.

2. *The above, plus. a major effort by the U.S. to arrange an international embargo blocking Iran's importation of badly needed non-food supplies, the optimum target being Iran's gasoline imports; and blocking Iran's exports of unrefined petroleum, the source of most of the country's revenues.*

Assessment: While it would be an effective punitive measure, this approach would also fail, as there is simply not enough international support for such measures, particularly from the EU and Japan.

3. *Impose a strong unilateral U.S. naval blockade of the country, while at the same time taking unilateral steps to*

shut off Iran's imports/exports by means other than through its Persian Gulf ports. This action would have immediate and significant impact on Iran. Given the political will to go at it alone, blockade by U.S. naval and air assets could deal a severe blow to Iran's economy.

Assessment: International reaction to such a step would be immediate and negative. Nor would our blockade necessarily prompt the Iranian Government to abandon its nuclear weapons program to ameliorate the adverse effects the blockade would have on its population. In fact, it might mobilize public support for the troubled Iranian government, and lead to a period of enthusiastic national belt-tightening during which Iran moved even more rapidly toward weapons acquisition. It could easily do this with increased assistance from North Korea.

We must assume that NO U.S. blockade would be able to stop the transport of nuclear weapons and/or components from North Korea to Iran, particularly since it is safe to assume that most such items can be moved by cargo aircraft. Further, it is likely that either (or both) Russia or China would probably agree to facilitate these air movements.

Finally, I have seen no evidence to suggest that this Administration would be willing to exercise this option – particularly in the wake of President Obama's absolutely stunning announcement that he intends to abandon the placement in Eastern Europe of missile defense systems targeted against Iran.

4.   *Mount unilateral U.S. air attacks on Iran's key nuclear-weapons related targets. This option is available only if our intelligence is good enough that we can with a high degree of certainty identify most of these targets. Assuming adequate intelligence, such attacks would have a very high possibility of success, and, in the medium term at least, would disable Iran's nuclear program.*

NOTE: Once Iran has actually manufactured nuclear weapons and has placed them in storage, the air attack option disappears. We would stand virtually no chance of identifying Iran's weapons storage locations, as opposed to its much larger manufacturing facilities. If preemptive air strikes against Iranian nuclear targets are to be mounted, they must be mounted very soon.

Assessment: In many ways this would be the most effective and quickest way to bring a halt to Iran's domestic nuclear weapons program. There are, however, risks:

A. It would do nothing to halt the possibility of Iran's simply buying nuclear weapons from North Korea.

B. Iran would certainly retaliate by increasing its support for the insurgents in Afghanistan, where the President is apparently bent on increasing our presence. Based on my experience in supporting the Afghan "Freedom Fighters" against the Soviet Union, I confidently believe that such support would, at a minimum, negate any advantages of the troop build-up. On the other hand, I believe that Iran has already decided to do this, so it is probably not a particularly significant or new issue.

C. Iran would probably retaliate by leaning on its Hezbollah surrogates in Lebanon to resume their highly effective attacks on Israel.

D. Iran would certainly redouble its efforts to destabilize Iraq - making it even less likely that Iraq can survive the full American troop withdrawal as a viable nation.

5. *Persuade Israel to make the above air attacks, and then clandestinely assist them to do so. For starters, this would mean providing them with our best intelligence; specialized ordnance and aircraft (including weapons optimized for deep-earth bunker destruction); refueling (in-flight or at our bases in Iraq); and more air defense weapons and aircraft to resist an expected Iranian response. In theory Israel has the most to lose if Iran obtains nuclear weapons; has a track record of doing exactly this sort of mission against foreign nuclear targets; and could not earn any more negative publicity and Iranian/Arab World enmity than it already has. In fact, the Israelis have carefully ensured that the world believes in the possibility of their unilaterally attacking Iran.*

Assessment: Note that I used the word "persuade" Israel to attack. Despite their deep fear of a nuclear-armed Iran and belligerent posture, I do not believe that Israel (with the exception noted below) would actually attack Iran - either on its own or as a result of our heavy bribes. The reason is Hezbollah, which very recently more or less "won" a brief war with Israel. An all-out and prolonged Hezbollah assault supported by extensive Iranian weapons (primarily missile) re-supply - and probably by the introduction of significant numbers of Iranian Revolutionary Guard and Palestinian "volunteers" - would inflict devastating and unacceptable damage on Israel.

Further, Iran has an Air Force and a Navy; probably could quickly obtain offensive missiles capable of hitting Israeli targets; and may well have chemical weapons. Where did the poison gas found by the U.N. in Saddam-era Iraq go? Probably Syria. Does anyone doubt that the Syrians would be happy to give such weapons to Iran in a fight with Israel? Or doubt the possibility that Syria itself would join up with Iran and Hezbollah to fight Israel?

The exception: There is every reason to believe that the Israelis, while fully cognizant of the great dangers posed by air attacks on Iran, could chose to accept the risks in a vaguely "doomsday" scenario. Make the air attacks; expect and respond as best as possible to the Iranian/Hezbollah/Syrian retaliation; refuse any mediation efforts by anyone, and, in the event that it appears that the existence of Israel itself is threatened, call upon the United States to enter the war on its side, which, with a high degree of certainty, the U.S. would do.

6. *Do none of the above, and come to terms with a nuclear armed Iran.*

My analysis of options 1 – 5 above is that none are either effective or worth attempting. I believe that the U.S. must accept Iran as a nuclear power: exactly as it has accepted North Korea and Pakistan.

This means that Iran will soon join the "Mutually Assured Destruction" (MAD) group of nations. History, so far, has shown that the existence of this group does not mean wars will break out. On the contrary, as our experience with China, Russia, and - so far - North Korea has shown it has probably averted wars. It certainly prevented the Cold War from becoming a catastrophic conventional-to-nuclear conflict. The Iranian Government is crazy, but not insane, and recognizes that an American (and/or Israeli) nuclear attack would destroy their country and themselves.

In the end, the U.S. can guarantee certain friends and/or allies from direct external attack, nuclear or conventional, by placing them under the same "nuclear umbrella" which won the Cold War in Europe and has allowed Japan and South Korea to prosper. Thus. the Saudis and various. other states important to U.S. can be protected from Iranian nuclear attack.

It would have been better had the U.S. and other nations forced North Korea and Iran to remain outside the nuclear club. That did not happen, as much as anything because of the lack of international support for U.S. efforts, so we must realistically face the situation we are in.

This, I believe, means that we must completely revisit how we deal with Iran. The first step is to deny the Mullahs their use of the U.S. stance on the nuclear issue to fan internal support.

We can be sure, as a result of the Iranian Government's acute domestic political need for a "foreign devil" to help sustain its brutal and illegitimate government that the U.S. will continue to be the target of Iranian vituperation. Our best response to that is indifference. Iran will continue to support terrorism wherever it suits its purposes, and we must continue to fight that nasty and difficult battle.

Our goal should be to provide support to the opponents of the Mullah dictatorship, so that at the end of the day Iranians themselves will destroy it. This will require subtlety, and action in extremely close cooperation with the EU. The past months have shown that there is an enormous reservoir of anti-Mullah feeling in the country: our game plan should be to deftly support that opposition. Iran is now in many ways a metaphor for Hitler's pre-WW Two Germany and the Soviet Union under Stalin. It will take time, but history shows that time is on the side of the Iranian people - and us.

Wednesday,
September 23, 2009

McChrystal's New Tactics

Over the past weeks two new tactical decisions have been made by General Stan McChrystal, the senior U.S./NATO commander in Afghanistan. The first of these was to announce a major change in the disposition of U.S./NATO troops: in effect spreading them thinly across the country. Based on my experience in fighting the Soviets in the 1980-1984 periods, I objected strongly in a previous article to this stratagem, basically since I know that it would result in much higher casualties to U.S. troops. I read today in the Washington Post that McChrystal has reversed this tactic and will now concentrate our troops in "urban areas". This is a significant change, and one for the better.

The second is McChrystal's directive that restricts the military's use of air strikes and artillery in order to reduce "collateral damage" amongst Afghan civilians. While I fully understand the reasoning behind this mandate – i.e., saving non combatant lives and avoiding the ill will of the population – it carries a very serious price. The policy, if carried out, is sure to increase the number of U.S. fatalities.

The fact is it is difficult to be a little bit pregnant in war; you either are or you are not. You are either fighting full bore or with your hands tied behind your back.

Tuesday, September 29, 2009

The McChrystal Report

Note: I have written at length on many aspects of the war in Afghanistan, trying to identify the realities that make impossible and unwarranted our commitment to militarily dominate that country - while at the same time undertaking huge nation-building efforts. These articles are posted on my blog at http://ciahart.blogspot.com. I particularly recommend "The Third Afghan War - Failed Strategies" and "The Third Afghan War - Part Two." At the risk of sounding like I am beating my own drum, I believe that it will benefit readers to know that, unlike almost all other commentators on this war - from academia, the press, Congress and civilians in this and the previous Administration - I spent three long years (in the midst of a war against the Soviets) working with and learning about the Afghans we are now fighting.

Gen. McChrystal's "Initial Assessment" is a brilliant piece of military staff work.

It absolutely validates French World War I Premiere Georges Clemenceau's maxim that "war is too important to be left to the generals."

In my view the report, which addresses President Obama's March 2009 strategic decision on Afghanistan, can be regarded as one of two things:

1. An attempt to pressure the President to radically and immediately increase U.S. troop strength in the belief that in a period of a year or so (a) a largely phantom Afghan Army and Afghan National Police Force can be created to save the

day militarily; (b) serious (and clearly visible to the population) progress can be made to reform every level of today's incredibly corrupt and despised Afghan governments; and (c) peace and safety can be brought to much larger segments of the population, thus building support for that government.

And, by stating that if all this is NOT done NOW, our chance of winning the war will be lost - the report provides a built-in exit strategy: defeat.

OR

2.   A disingenuous effort, using some accomplished "dazzle the President with bullshit," to tell him that if you will please read between the lines the war cannot be won.

I am a proponent of leaving Afghanistan now, shifting our focus to helping defend and repair Pakistan (which, unlike Afghanistan, does matter), and "surgically" fighting such elements of al-Qaeda as may return to a Taliban-dominated Afghanistan from Pakistan and carriers at sea.

If (2.) above is the case, I hope that some sharp eye in the White House will see between the lines.

If (1.) is the case, it provides a strategy built on sand, reinforced by self-deception that WILL fail.

The following are my comments on key issues raised - or ignored - by the McChrystal report. They are necessarily brief: any one of these issues could be debated with near-theological intensity. It is, however, not necessary to discuss how many Afghan (or other) angels can dance on the head of a pin: I submit it is necessary to make a handful of fundamental assessments which lead to fundamental decisions: then fret over the details.

The Rationale for War

Before one can comment on the report, which addresses what Gen. McChrystal believes we must do to win the war after years of failure, we must first question the President's March 2009 underlying premise: that Afghanistan is a "necessary war" which MUST be fought and won in order to prevent al-Qaeda from returning and using it as a base for future operations against us. To do this, Mr. Obama believes that we must achieve military dominance over the country; establish a capable and functioning Afghan government; and provide enormous quantities of economic assistance that will in theory build popular support for that government.

I believe that this rationale, which the Bush Administration established eight years ago and which President Obama thus far appears to accept, is deadly wrong. Eight years ago we invaded a country much larger than Iraq, with a much larger population (of perhaps 44 million people), to rid the country of, at most, a few thousand al-Qaeda terrorists. We successfully drove this handful of Arab and Pakistani terrorists into Pakistan, where they remain. We then chose to take on the Taliban, which is made up of Afghans and which more or less controlled the country, on the theory that if we did not destroy that radical Islamic Afghan organization, al-Qaeda would return. And we have been fighting Afghans - both Taliban and non-Taliban - with ever diminishing success ever since.

There has been a recent glimmer of hope suggesting that the President may be backing away from his "war of necessity" stance: the strategy for which Gen. McChrystal wrote the report. Last Sunday Secretary of Defense Bob Gates stated that the President is now working to ensure that the "right strategy" is in place. If the President is indeed reviewing his policy decision of earlier this year, I can only hope that he concludes that the policy he enunciated in March is NOT the correct path to follow.

The war in Afghanistan is being fought against the wrong enemy - the Taliban and other Afghan insurgent groups - only because we choose to be there to fight them. We have managed to forget that no matter how obscene and distasteful the Taliban is and was, it posed no threat to the United States (in fact we happily ignored them for years), and they had no quarrel with U.S. as of the time we invaded their country. Yet we justify our being there, fighting (and losing) an all-out war with them, on the presumption that al-Qaeda will return if we are not there. And that if they do, we can only fight them if we control the entire country.

The terrorists who mounted the 9/11 attacks in New York were not Afghans, and were not recruited or trained in Afghanistan, so 9/11 of itself can no longer serve to justify this war. I was astounded when a supporter of our continued fighting, writing in a major U.S. newspaper, recently justified the war on the absurd grounds that it is "enough that the 9/11 attacks were conceived" by al-Qaeda in Afghanistan.

Al-Qaeda has long since found sanctuary in Pakistan, and has grown and spread to other countries. It has proven that it does not need Afghanistan, and its supporters have been trained in Pakistan and in Africa. To say that we have no choice except to continue to occupy and fight for an entire country - that we are in a "necessary war" in and for Afghanistan - in order to deny bases to a handful of al-Qaeda terrorists, was wrong when it was first mooted by the Bush Administration, and is even more wrong now that we have experienced eight years of failure in attempting to do it.

Finally, supporters of the war in the Administration and Congress have begun to sound the facile but utterly fallacious Vietnam era type mantra to the effect that we cannot leave Afghanistan because to do so would demonstrate that we do not have the national will to stay the course against terrorism; that we would be abandoning our (undefined) "friends"; that we would give al-Qaeda a psychological "victory"; and that we would have no means to fight al-Qaeda if it returned to a Taliban-run Afghanistan. I call this the "Vietnam Fallacy".

Except for the last, every one of these assertions is directly and exactly parallel to the justifications that extended our tragic stay in Vietnam - and are exactly as invalid in this situation as they were then. Particularly in the wake of our declared intent to depart from Iraq, where one can hardly say that our goals - many of them similar to those proposed for Afghanistan - have not been met. The Vietnam War was regarded as an American defeat. We survived. The Arab and most of the rest of the world regard Iraq as an American defeat: we survive. If we withdraw from Afghanistan we will survive.

In fact, I believe that not withdrawing NOW will see U.S. withdrawing later, with the added tragedy of having spent more lives and money.

Finally, please remember that we are NOT fighting al-Qaeda in Afghanistan: we are fighting Afghans who are fighting for their country.

Nor is it true that leaving Afghanistan means we would necessarily abandon fighting al-Qaeda. We should be fighting them in Pakistan by supporting that country, and can continue fighting them in Afghanistan by using much more selective methods FROM Pakistan and the high seas.

McChrystal's Report

As I stated in my opening paragraph, I find the report brilliant in that it appears to take a hard and calculating look at the war – but in many key areas it actually does not. It also does not address several vital issues. In many instances, the report proposes solutions that (if implemented immediately) will allegedly save the day - solutions that realistically are not possible. Because of several serious omissions and dubious assumptions I think that it does the President and the country a grave disservice.

For example, the report places extraordinary emphasis on creating much larger and more effective Afghan Army and Police forces, which it states are absolutely fundamental to our long term success. It then basically states that we have about ONE year to accomplish much of this build-up in order to reverse the tide of war, after which continued expansion of Afghan forces will enable us to go on to "win."

The effort to raise a large, well trained and effective Afghan Army has been underway for years, with considerable lack of success. The report does not explain why. Worse, it largely assumes that raising such forces, AND being able to rely on them, can be accomplished: when in fact, recent history and the nature of the Afghan tribal both indicate that the effort is probably impossible.

The report does not adequately address and analyze the nature of the enemy we are fighting - which, when you come right down to it, happens to be THE major factor in this war. While briefly acknowledging that "the enemy" is a tough nut, it pretty much leaves it at that. Yet the very nature of the Afghan insurgent, and the population as a whole, will, in the end, decide whether we can or cannot win the land war we are fighting in Afghanistan. I do not know whether this is intentional or reflects a lack of understanding: either way, it is a huge disservice to the policy maker. The fact is that the Afghan warrior is an extraordinary enemy, whose courage; determination and resiliency make him an unusually difficult foe.

The report does not begin to address the size and nature of the economic development and nation building aspects of the war; aspects that are at least as important as combat operations. Are we and/or NATO really prepared to invest the many billions of dollars that are necessary to bring about nothing less than an economic miracle in one of the most poverty stricken countries in the world? If the economic development "war" is not McChrystal's direct responsibility, whose is it? What, if anything, has been estimated and planned in this area? How can McChrystal plan and fight a war without having those calculations in hand? All of this is unanswered.

The report also does not address the very severe collateral damage that the continuation and expansion of the war will have on Pakistan, a country that all agree MUST not be allowed to collapse. It may be that his instructions forbade him to address these considerations. Whatever the reason, this omission leaves the proposals to stand on their own – a fatal error.

There is only the most cursory mention of the grave implications of increased clandestine Iranian support for the insurgents. This may be contained in a classified annex. On the other hand, it certainly must be made known to the public that the Iranians have been providing assistance to the insurgents, and, in the light of the U.S.'s adversarial position with Iran over nuclear issues, it is reasonable to expect such Iranian assistance will grow rapidly in the future. Iran will become to this insurgency what Pakistan was to the anti-Soviet insurgency. Such covert assistance will come not only in the provision of more and better weapons to fight us, but will include some masterful and much-needed strategic advice which will assist the Taliban to challenge our forces. For example, I have been told by reliable Pakistani sources that recent Taliban activity outside of its normal areas of operations in Afghanistan was proposed by Iranian "advisors". Covert Iranian assistance has been responsible for the deaths of many American soldiers in Iraq: as it has been so far on a smaller scale in Afghanistan. It is an absolute certainty that the Iranians will greatly increase their assistance to the insurgents, who will in effect be Iran's surrogate killers of U.S. soldiers.

There is no mention in the report of the possibility of negotiating with the Taliban and/or non-Taliban insurgent groups. This too may be the subject of a classified annex, but for those of us not privy to such an annex – if there is one – it is important to raise the possibilities afforded by such discussions. While this is an exceedingly complex issue, we must remember that for centuries tribal allegiances have been purchased. There are areas, particularly in southeastern Afghanistan, where independent warlords may very well be bought off for, if nothing else, their neutrality. Dealing with the Taliban is infinitely more complex, but it is imperative that we meet with key Taliban leaders to explore possibilities of some kind of truce. Put another way, it is ridiculous to simply regard the Taliban as a sworn enemy and not to attempt to arrive at "certain understandings" with them. Duplicity is every Afghan's middle name and a Golden Rule amongst the Tribals. We might as well try to take advantage of that trait.

Finally, the report does not pay sufficient attention to the NATO contribution. While I realize that this is a political issue, I believe that McChrystal would have been within his rights to have factored in a serious assessment of how the presence or absence of NATO forces, and their roles and numbers, would impact on his recommendations and the future course of events. He knows that the EU turned down President Obama's request for additional troops months ago, and that domestic pressures on NATO allies to remove their troops are growing; largely because troops from key NATO contributors (excepting Britain) have only recently begun to be involved in the war, and are taking casualties, however minimal, for the first time. McChrystal, as the senior NATO commander in-country, surely could and should have made estimative comments on the consequences of NATO force increases/decreases. This is a serious deficiency, particularly since our NATO allies are themselves carefully reading the report, on which they will no doubt partly base their decisions on their contribution to a future war.

Comment: Here are the major realities that I believe must be in kept mind when reading the report and, more importantly, when trying to make use of it in deciding whether to raise the stakes in the battle for Afghanistan OR to abandon the war.

A.   Can we defeat the insurgency militarily?

Assuming that the Administration and NATO does not increase overall troop strength in Afghanistan to a level of around 400,000 men, I believe the answer is an unequivocal NO. I did NOT pull that number from thin air. Having played an important and direct role in the First Afghan War (against the Soviets), I am keenly aware of the problems that faced the Soviet 40th Army commander in Afghanistan when he was fighting that insurgency - and was limited to having about 140,000 Soviet troops in the country. The 400,000 number surfaced (after the collapse of the Soviet Union) as having been submitted to the Kremlin, and denied. Then we have the U.S. Army's own COIN (counter-insurgency) manual: prepared under the direction of General David Petraeus, who now runs Central Command - with Afghanistan falling in his purview. This is the Army's "bible" for fighting a major counter-insurgency. It calls for troop strength that varies directly with the size of the population where the counter-insurgency is fought: 400,000 men is almost exactly the number specified by the formula in that manual - which presumably is the product of the best thinking on the subject in the U.S. military. Absolutely no one suggests that U.S./NATO force levels could or should be expanded to anything near this number. Even assuming that the President were to authorize as many as 150,000 U.S. troops, and that our NATO allies do not remove their limited troop contributions (as it appears they are increasingly inclined to do), we will never have enough military strength on the ground.

Nor can the total strength of friendly forces be raised by depending on the assumption that very large numbers of Afghan Army forces can be raised, trained and relied upon. As I have previoU.S.ly noted, this is wishful thinking rooted in our Western concepts of a nation-state. Afghanistan is not a nation; has never had a national government; and has never accepted even the concept of a National Army. It is a tribal society which has always fought its wars, internal and against external invaders, on the basis of strong ethnic, regional and tribal loyalties. Many centuries of deeply-held regional, ethnic, linguistic and tribal hatreds make the creation of a National Army impossible. Even if a large number of men were to be recruited, trained, and labeled an "Afghan National Army," the inevitable pull of tribal and ethnic loyalties will override any superficial commitment to a non-existent "nation" and "government," and bring about its rapid disintegration.

I believe, exactly as happened to the 80,000-strong Soviet-trained "Afghan Army" that existed when the anti-Soviet insurgency was launched, that most of any army we raise will quickly melt away.

We will in fact be training large numbers of men who will in the end join the insurgency against U.S.; men who will refuse to fight where and when they do not want to; men whose basic loyalty to money - after their tribe and ethnic ties – lasts only as long as it is convenient to them; men born and raised in a culture of savage duplicity; men who fundamentally regard us with a mix of contempt and dislike because we are "infidels", and for that reason often willingly respond to the pull of radical Islam; and men who have no loyalty whatever to governments, foreigners, or what we call democratic ideals.

For these reasons I submit that Gen. McChrystal's plan, with its overwhelming dependence on raising an effective Afghan Army and Police force, is a prescription for failure.

B.   Is it reasonable to expect continued popular or Congressional
Support for the War?

While I have no special qualifications to address this issue, it certainly looks to me that developments in the Congressional Democratic Party and in public opinion polls over the past months strongly suggest that the President cannot reasonably expect that Congress or the American people will support keeping large numbers of U.S. troops in Afghanistan for many years. As recently mooted by Secretary of Defense Gates, this could be for at least ten years -a number with which I fully agree. Without such long-term support our forces might have one or two years before Congressional and/or public support dries up and they are withdrawn: a time period that is ludicrously short given the task at hand. Every American life lost in that period is, in effect, deliberately thrown away.

It is now President Obama's war - no longer a Bush legacy. I can only wonder whether the President is willing to risk his popularity and Congressional support on a war that at the very least is of doubtful outcome. And of even more doubtful necessity.

Comment: Congressional Republican support for the war remains strong – largely because of loyalty to ex-President Bush and their adherence to the "Vietnam Fallacy" I discuss above. While Democrats control both houses, and ultimate decisions on war rest in their hands because they "own" the money, it would no doubt help the Democrats to stand up against President Obama on the war issue if at least some Republicans broke party discipline and joined with anti-war Democrats.

C.   How determined are our Afghan enemies to fight a long war?

Afghan insurgents, Taliban and others, continue to demonstrate that they are ferociously determined to fight foreign invaders. And they are doing so with increasingly sophisticated weapons and tactics, with resultant increases in our personnel losses. While many Americans have tended to look at our mission in Afghanistan as one of "liberation," bringing social and economic improvement, nearly all Afghans regard it as an unwarranted invasion which has already brought them eight years of war - and threatens to bring them more. These insurgents will never give up, and as General McChrystal reports, their increasing numbers, improving skills, tenacity and willingness to fight are all too evident.

Fighting a successful counter-insurgency requires having reasonably effective and honest central and regional governments that people believe are worth supporting, and around which they and government military forces can rally. As I have previously written, there has never been even a semi-effective central government in Afghanistan, and regional governments have traditionally been virtually independent fiefdoms: corruption has been the rule at all levels. Thirty years of war has turned this long-ineffective government structure into little more than a means to organize the distribution of spoils and to legitimize the authority of local powers-that-be. The central government of President Karzai, and the regional governments under him, are regarded by the populace as foreign puppets which have taken corruption and inefficiency to new heights. Which is true, and is a situation wildly beyond our ability to correct. This plays a key role in denying U.S. the support of the already war-weary population, as does our noble but self-defeating attempt to destroy the only worthwhile cash crop in the country – the opium poppy.

Comment: I was amazed at the level of surprise and concern evinced in both the U.S. and Europe over the vast corruption associated with the recent Afghan elections. To me such corruption was absolutely inevitable, a staple fixture of how things are done in Afghanistan, and absolutely predictable. Frankly, if the degree of corruption was really an eye-opener to many, it served a good purpose by providing a clear example of the real state of affairs in the country.

Finally, we must remember that in the eyes of the population (and the Taliban) we are the aggressors, and that our invasion of Afghanistan was in no way justified by the fact that the Taliban allowed a tiny group of al-Qaeda terrorists to operate training bases in the country. Further, now that al-Qaeda is gone, most Afghans see no justification whatever for our remaining in their country. The Taliban and the other insurgents fighting against us do so because we are in their territory, intervening in their affairs, killing their people. All insurgent groups draw support (and recruits) by simply pointing to the basic injustice of our presence, and to our determination to wage war against them. In their eyes we are just another in a long series of foreign invaders who, for reasons of our own, arrived to fight them for their land. And who, as always, can and will be defeated. Add to this the power of Islamic beliefs and our status with the mass of the population as infidels and unbelievers, we do not and will not have extensive popular support.

If we withdraw from Afghanistan we most emphatically could run effective operations against al-Qaeda from Pakistan and elsewhere. We have long since established effective working relationships with the Pakistan Army, and I have been told by my senior retired Pakistani military contacts that Pakistan would allow U.S. to base small numbers of Special Forces troops and their necessary helicopter support, dedicated to missions inside Afghanistan, in remote locations in Pakistan near the Afghan border. In their view this is vastly preferable to our continuing - and perhaps expanding - the general war in Afghanistan: a war that has created enormous difficulties in Pakistan. Such units could provide quick reaction capabilities for raids into Afghanistan if it were necessary to make small scale surgical attacks on al-Qaeda targets - if any turned up. Air support for the Special Forces elements could be provided by carrier based aircraft, thus eliminating the need to base piloted strike or reconnaissance aircraft in Pakistan. We already have Pakistan-based facilities to support anti-terrorist activities, just as we have established and effective joint intelligence and tactical operations command centers in Pakistan. I am not suggesting that fighting al-Qaeda - IF it returns to Afghanistan after we withdraw - would be easy. Nothing is: but it is within our military's capability; much of the infrastructure in Pakistan already exists; and it would be infinitely more sensible and cost effective - in terms of blood and money - than fighting in and for all of Afghanistan.

D. Which matters more: Pakistan or Afghanistan?

At face value, the question is almost absurd: Pakistan, of course. Eight years of war in Afghanistan resulted in our exporting both al-Qaeda and the Taliban to Pakistan, with enormously disruptive consequences. If we continue the war there is every reason to believe that instability in Pakistan will increase: indeed Pakistan's very existence as a moderate, nuclear-armed Muslim nation will be called into question. My sources in Pakistan, retired senior military and intelligence officers, tell me that the Pakistan Army leadership believes that the U.S. is making an investment in blood and money "on the wrong side of the border", and is "dragging us down with them." They believe that it would be a major error for the U.S. and NATO to remain in Afghanistan. They note that the Taliban not only survived the American invasion of 2001, thereafter moving in strength into Pakistan, but has grown in strength, effectiveness and ambition. In their view the Taliban has "fought the Americans to a losing position" in Afghanistan, and now challenges Pakistan itself. Further, in a radical change of position, the Army now thinks that the best way and place to fight the Taliban is in Pakistan.

In their view, however, Pakistan's military cannot solve the problems on its Frontier with Afghanistan on its own. The Army's dilemma is that even though it has military forces, it does not have the necessary back-up that must be provided by really extensive economic development in the Frontier; their notion being that the Pushtuns require, as always, a mix of military pressure and bribes, which in this case means economic development.

It should be understood that in the case of the Frontier, economic development means the rapid provision of the basic amenities and conveniences that immediately improve the lives of the locals. For example, the appearance of many dozens of properly staffed and equipped medical clinics; new wells to provide fresh water supplies, electricity, and the provision of new and better roads in the Frontier would be a tangible demonstration of the fact that avoiding the Taliban has its rewards. In other words, enormous construction projects that require years to complete are not at this point what is needed. Many small, eminently feasible, highly visible and relatively inexpensive projects, each of which quickly and significantly improves the lives of the local Pushtuns, will do the trick.

There are allegations, including in the McChrystal report, that Pakistan's military intelligence service (ISI), even while playing a key role in fighting the Taliban in Pakistan, maintains discreet contacts with the Taliban. Of course it does. It must. Because Pakistan quite reasonably cannot place its full faith and confidence in the U.S. – particularly in regards to our staying the course with Pakistan. The history of Pak-U.S. relations is such that the Pakistanis would be fools to believe that we are truly in a long-term "do all that it takes" relationship with them. Every worthwhile intelligence service keeps a "few lines open" to an enemy: contacts that might prove indispensable in a rapidly changing situation. Further, such contacts often provide an excellent means to obtain information about the enemy. What matters is whether ISI truly supports Pakistan's present campaign against its internal insurgencies: my sources are adamant that it does.

Summary

I think we should be prepared to accept an Afghanistan that is dominated and run by the Taliban. We are under no obligation, moral or otherwise, to "free" Afghanistan from the Taliban, no matter how egregious it is. If we are so arrogant as to believe that the United States is morally obliged to take on and "remediate" all of the savage dictatorships of the world, there are more promising candidates on a long list of countries. We have lived with the Taliban in control of Afghanistan before; we can do so again.

Nor must we fall into a trap of our own making: the view that we must remain in Afghanistan in order to do battle with our real enemy: al-Qaeda. Consider: if, after enormous expense in men and money, we were to prevail in Afghanistan, AND succeed in helping to drive them from Pakistan as well, is it reasonable to think that we will have destroyed al-Qaeda?

NO.

That terrorist organization will long since have moved to a more amenable location (or locations).

It is likely that we will be at war with al-Qaeda and similar radical Islamic terrorist organizations far into the future. Success in that long war will depend on many things, among them good intelligence; good strategy and tactics; world-wide cooperation with other nations; and a nimble and properly trained military.

Being stuck in one vast hole into which we throw our resources, build the enmity of the Muslim world, risk isolating ourselves from our nominal allies, and probably can't win, is foolish.

As is obvious from the above, there is no end to the traps and pitfalls in the Afghan issue. At the end of the day, however, we have to trust in the common sense and integrity of men like Secretary of Defense Bob Gates and the Chairman of the Joint Chiefs of Staff, Admiral Mike Mullen. They, unlike the White House and much of Congress, have memories of the dreadful lessons of Vietnam, with which there are so many parallels as we consider Afghanistan.

Friday, October 9, 2009

Afghanistan Part Three: Basic Decisions and Unknown Goals

If various newspaper reporters are right, the President has made the decision that he does not intend to reduce troop levels in Afghanistan in the near term, and all that remains to be decided is how many - if any- additional troops should be sent in response to General McChrystal's request for more resources.

It appears that in the course of the current White House policy review there have been some glimmers of recognition that fighting the Taliban for all of Afghanistan in order to deny al-Qaeda a future operations base may not be a sound concept. But the President's policy appears to be to continue to do just that. This will, apparently, continue to be a "war of necessity," and Gen. McChrystal will, presumably, get some additional troops.

The President's decision is, I assume, driven by the idea that by hanging on in Afghanistan two of General McChrystal's major goals: building a large and effective Afghan Army and Police force (to replace U.S. soldiers); and cleaning up the country's incredibly corrupt government (to earn the support of the population) can be achieved.

So, it appears we are in for more of the same for at least the next year or so.

There is one major difference: McChrystal plans to abandon efforts to seek out and destroy the Taliban, and will concentrate on "providing security" for Afghan cities and towns.

That shift in strategy on troop dispositions should result in a) significantly fewer Taliban casualties, and b) significantly fewer U.S. casualties. It also means that the Taliban will pretty much have a blank check to operate throughout the rest of the country. That is very good news for the Taliban, since, among other things, it effectively gives them safe havens in Afghanistan while they continue their attacks in Pakistan. And, perhaps, over the long term, it is good news for U.S., since the fewer casualties we take while achieving (or not achieving) the above goals the better.

These are conflicting and confusing developments which can be boiled down to one major question: what are the President's ultimate goals?

> Is it still his objective to destroy the Taliban in Afghanistan and build an economically improved, "moderate" country: this to be achieved by "hanging on" until an Afghan National Army and Police can be raised to do the job with and for us?

If so, he is making a number of terribly risky (and I believe, flawed) assumptions, among them: a) the war in Afghanistan is necessary to "defeat" al-Qaeda; b) the still-mythical Afghan Army and Police can be created and relied upon; c) Congress and the American public will stay the course; d) NATO will stay with us; and e) Pakistan will not be irretrievably damaged in the process.

> Is he merely temporizing, thus delaying the acknowledgment of what years of war have shown U.S.: we cannot "win" in Afghanistan – at least without committing a huge number of American (and NATO) troops and spending billions in economic aid over a period of many years?

Gen. McChrystal has taken a very brave step by forcing the President to confront the military aspects of the Afghan issue. Since, in Washington, no good deed goes unpunished, he will probably pay for it.

If he is to be a wartime President, Obama must display leadership – not just rely on platitudes and consensus-driven strategy. The country should demand a clear statement from the President on his goals, which he must justify in the cold light of reality. That is the least he must do before he continues and/or expands this war.

Tuesday, October 13, 2009

Afghanistan Part Four: Leaving Afghanistan, A Modest Proposal

1. Let us assume that the Administration reaches the following conclusions in its current review of the Afghan War:

    A. The Taliban is NOT our enemy in the war on terror. Thus it is neither necessary nor desirable to remain in Afghanistan for an indefinite period, fighting an endless battle against the Taliban and others, in order to continue the war against al-Qaeda, which, as a practical matter, no longer exists in Afghanistan.

    B. Prospects are dim for raising, within the next two or three years, a large and effective Afghan National Army and Police for the purpose of assisting U.S. in fighting the Taliban. Equally dim are the chances in that period that an incredibly corrupt and detested central government can be significantly reformed and gain the support of the Afghan people.

    C. The growing strength of the Taliban in both Pakistan and Afghanistan, and ever-more frequent and effective Taliban attacks on the Pakistani Government, will increasingly threaten the stability of that already deeply troubled country. We must focus on helping Pakistan defend itself against both the Afghan Taliban and the growing threat of domestic Islamic radicalism. That is where we should place our emphasis.

    D. The most effective way to reduce the Taliban threat to Pakistan is to take the pressure off the Taliban in Afghanistan so that it will voluntarily return to its own territory, which is where its interests lie.

    E. Our battle against al-Qaeda in Afghanistan can be continued by small numbers of U.S. Special Forces operating from remote border areas in Pakistan, supported by carrier based aircraft; plus continued intelligence and military support and cooperation with Pakistan.

2. If the above conclusions are accepted as the background for policy formulation, it is necessary to develop a strategy to accomplish that policy. The following is a modest proposal for that strategy.

    A. Working in concert with our NATO allies, we should announce to all Afghans, particularly the Taliban, that we will no longer fight an all-out war to determine who runs their country, and how. However, we will remain in the country for one additional year, long enough to enable Afghans to exercise their rights of self-determination by creating a "new Afghanistan."

    B. Our intent (following Gen. McChrystal's current theory) is to withdraw from the countryside, and to provide security only for the main cities and major towns for a period of one year, after which all NATO forces will be withdrawn. U.S. and NATO troops will NOT seek combat with Taliban or other insurgent forces in that year, but WILL aggressively defend the cities and towns in order to protect the population therein, and to allow the following steps to be accomplished:

        1. In the course of the year, arrangements, overseen by UN observers, will be made by representatives of all major groups - including the Taliban – to hold a National "Jirga" (assembly), which will be charged with producing a new Constitution for the country.

        2. This will be followed by national elections for new governments at the Central and Provincial levels.

        3. Immediately after those elections are held, all NATO forces will be withdrawn from the country.

        4. Since we will be adopting a purely defensive policy in the country, for a very limited time, NO additional U.S. or NATO troops need by sent.

Comment: There are, obviously, many possible impediments to the plan. For example, the Taliban may choose NOT to participate in the Jirga and/or the elections. If it does participate, it may seek to use brute force to influence the outcome of the voting in those areas of the country where it holds sway – as will other armed elements in other areas. The country may collapse (whatever that means) once U.S./NATO forces are finally withdrawn.

The plan should, however, go forward.

It is neither our moral obligation nor a national security requirement to create some vestige of a "real democracy" in Afghanistan, justified by saying that it is necessary to do so in order to defeat al-Qaeda. It is not. We have lived with an unstable Afghanistan before, and we can again. This has nothing whatever to do with our continuing to fight al-Qaeda and/or any other of the world's terrorist organizations.

The alternative, however, in as many years of warfare - meaning the expenditure of American lives and money we do not have - as the American people (to say nothing of our timorous NATO allies) and Congress are prepared to accept.

Not many years, I suspect. And every American life lost in that interim period will serve no purpose whatever.

Tuesday, October 27, 2009

A Troubling Conversation

I recently had a conversation with a very senior retired officer from a major European (continental) intelligence service. The subject of our conversation was Afghanistan.

While he was very discreet in phrasing his comments, he had two major points to pass along to me "off the record." The first was that his former Service has informed its political masters that it believes that a war in Afghanistan that seeks to defeat the Taliban is unwinnable unless the Americans radically increase their troop strength – and the NATO countries do the same. He added that he personally does not believe that his government is prepared to increase significantly its contribution to the Afghan war effort. His understanding is that his government's leadership is attempting to frame a negative response in the event President Obama decides to increase the level of U.S. forces and asks NATO to do the same.

The second point took me completely by surprise: analysts in his former Service believe that President Obama's dithering over a decision to increase U.S. forces or not, is actually intentional. They suggest that his purpose is to distract the American public from being able to focus exclusively on the emotionally charged and divisive national health care issue, which is his primary concern.

Comment: Whether or not this is correct, it is interesting that from at least one European perspective the President's apparent indecisiveness is in fact an intentional strategy to gain domestic political advantage.

Thursday, October 29, 2009

Dithering

A few days ago I placed an article on the Blog based on a conversation I had with a friend who is a retired European Intelligence officer. One of his comments was that his former Service had concluded that the explanation for President Obama's repeated delays in announcing his Afghan War policy is NOT repeat NOT because he is pondering the evidence before him. Their conclusion was that the President is in fact stalling because his Afghan decision is bound to anger Democrats whose votes he needs to pass the health care reform legislation now before Congress.

I have not heard or read any commentary in the media supporting my friend's assertion, but I have received replies from several readers stating that they have reliable sources in the White House and Congress who confirm the European's assessment. In effect, the President is holding a vital foreign policy decision hostage to an unrelated domestic agenda that is in deep trouble in Congress.

For several reasons I find this unconscionable. First, we are coming to the end of the bloodiest month of the eight-year conflict, with every indication that the increase in Taliban activity will continue. The war grows ever more deadly while the Taliban has greater success. This has been accompanied by a radical increase in terrorist activity in Pakistan. There is growing unhappiness amongst our troops in Afghanistan, who very much await The Presidential Word on the war they are fighting. Both NATO and the Pakistani government grow more nervous over American dithering.

Next, I assume that the President's delays are a consequence of his intention to announce that his fundamental decision (which he has already made) is to keep U.S. troops fighting in Afghanistan.

In other words, I suspect he has decided to do more of the same in Afghanistan - at a crucial moment when we could make a bold decision to extricate ourselves from an unwinnable war (which our military has essentially told him it is). He will justify this decision by saying that we will be introducing major strategic/tactical improvements on the ground. This, in my view, will not have major positive results.

Finally, if the President finds it necessary to avoid making this decision public because he needs the votes for health care, is he not simply delaying the inevitable: the rejection by Congress - and the public - of his new plan?

Friday, October 30, 2009

A Triumph for Usama bin Laden

In Rome's heyday, say around 100 B.C., a victorious Roman General returning from that most noble of Roman endeavors – invading, subjugating, looting, and rapeing a foreign territory – was granted a "Triumph." This was an extravaganza that could last for days, the point of which was to celebrate the General's great achievements in war. While Usama bin Laden will have no three-day bacchanal in Rome, he has every right to claim a "Triumph" for his success in his self-declared war against both the non-Muslim world, (the United States in particular) and much of the world that is Muslim.

Consider the objectives he set out for himself well over 10 years ago: to ignite and sustain a massive radical Islamic "jihad" (religious war) against the West and the governments of Muslim countries that do not meet his definition of being "Islamic." With regard to the United States, his frequently stated objective has been to destroy our society: our economy, our system of government and law, and our peaceful pursuit of our individual and national aspirations - killing as many Americans as possible along the way.

By any measure, bin Laden has been extraordinarily successful. He has, for example, drawn us into eight years of war (with perhaps more to come) in Afghanistan and, partly, in Iraq: wars we cannot afford in terms either of money or of lives expended. He has forced us to divert billions of dollars we don't have into domestic efforts to defend ourselves against the many threats posed by Islamic terrorists. In addition to the tragic deaths in New York on 9/11, and the thousands of American lives lost in the wars against this elusive target, he has brought us to fear the possibility of violent attacks everywhere in our own country. By doing so he has completely altered our behavior, lifestyle, and society. Every American considers himself or herself a potential target, inside our own borders: a potential victim of an invisible and incomprehensible enemy.

Bin Laden has placed America under siege: something four major 20th Century wars never did: a situation that would have been seen as unimaginable one short decade ago. He will never destroy our republic, but he has had a pervasive malignant effect on U.S..

His success has sparked the creation of a host of radical Islamic terrorist organizations which, taken together, are our enemy. The word "al-Qaeda" has evolved to represent a much broader collection of terrorist groups patterned on al-Qaeda but not led by Usama bin Laden. Today "al-Qaeda" is shorthand for radical Islamic groups around the world, which share bin Laden's vision and goals, and I use the "title" in that sense.

Bin Laden has had incredible impact from Cairo to Calcutta to Chicago: few individuals in history have had such an extraordinary effect on the world in such a short period of time. Even more amazing is the fact that he has had this success without the usual trappings of power: the backing of a nation-state and an organized military, etc. al-Qaeda's success is precisely the result of not having an identifiable geographic base. Our inability to understand this and our need to find – or create – some focal point to attack is what led U.S. to a full-scale war in Afghanistan. Our Western psyche has not been able to grasp that such a powerful adversary can and does exist and thrive in an amorphous world.

Usama bin Laden has earned his Triumph.

He has done this by unleashing the pent-up anger and frustration of millions of Muslims: transforming a moribund, largely politically irrelevant, and very slowly modernizing religion into a vehicle to justify and support a war against both "infidels" and moderate Muslim regimes. He has reawakened time-honored traditions of an aggressive (and fanatic) Islam as the engine to drive a new jihad. Very much as Ayatollah Khomeini and his successors in Iran have done, bin Laden has harnessed a religion to serve his own purposes.

Further, he has chosen to use the one weapon we cannot easily defend against: unremitting, indiscriminate, and savage terror. And terrorism, carried on long enough, works.

The conditions that have fostered this "Islamic resurgence," this crusade of Muslim terrorism, will not change in the foreseeable future. The al-Qaeda "factor" – in many guises - will be with us for decades.

My own sense is that we as a nation, and the western community of nations, are not dealing with the multiple parts of the "factor" in a coherent, coordinated, and realistic fashion. Among other things, we frustrate our counter terrorism efforts by insisting on playing by our rules against an enemy with no rules. Example: in the U.S., a political decision to close Guantanamo has created the very real possibility that bloodied terrorists will soon be set loose, and created a quandary over what to do with future captured terrorists. And interrogators are not only denied the tools to gather priceless intelligence from captured terrorists, but are to be prosecuted for their past work – clearly a political effort to drag the senior political leadership of a former Administration into court.

I see no evidence that this Administration has made any positive contributions to improving our defenses, and/or working with other nations to enhance/expand efforts against a mutual threat. A White House which wants to abandon the phrase "war on terror," and that is working to dismantle an awkward but sensible means to detain terrorists, generally seems oblivious to the uncompromising savagery of our enemies, and appears more interested in seeking to demonize the previous Administration than it does to actually seizing the problem and bringing renewed vigor and good sense to it.

Along with a steadily growing number of careful observers, I believe that facts repeat facts make clear that the Afghan war is both unnecessary and unwinnable. We are not fighting al-Qaeda terrorism in Afghanistan; we are fighting people who do not want U.S. in their country. We are in effect doing Usama bin Laden a great favor by diverting so many of our resources into a theatre which is irrelevant to domestic terrorist attacks. If I were Usama bin Laden I would want to see the United States endlessly mired in Afghanistan, burning up money and people with little effect on my own activities. This supports my assertion that America and Americans are "the enemy" of Islam, which brings me both new recruits and greater sympathy in the Muslim world. In addition, as bin Laden I would applaud the continued – and expanded – American presence in Afghanistan because it encourages ever more Taliban terrorism in Pakistan, which I encourage and support in order to destroy the moderate government of Pakistan, which at the moment is the most vulnerable of all Muslim states to take-over by radical Islam.

Because of the above, I have an uneasy feeling that this Administration's expected commitment to further fighting in Afghanistan may be a political move by the President to demonstrate his anti-terrorist bona fides. I assume that most Democrats wish to support "their" President – however reluctantly. I also assume such support is a near-term phenomenon, and will evaporate as casualty figures rise and visible successes diminish. Republicans appear to be hopelessly trapped in a knee-jerk pro-war mindset.

Al-Qaeda (in the sense the term is used above) will strike again in the United States. Recent arrests of conspirators planning such attacks vividly prove the point. I wonder if it will take another massive attack against a perfectly innocent non-combatant target in the U.S. to bring this Administration to understand that the real theatre of operations against al-Qaeda is here at home.

Let us not give Usama bin Laden another Triumph.

Monday, November 16, 2009

To War or Not to War (With Apologies to the Late Prince of Denmark)

It appears from press speculation and visits to Pakistan by Senator Hillary Clinton and National Security Advisor General James Jones, both of whom urged the Pakistanis to do more to fight the Taliban, which the President is close to announcing that he will continue the war, and will probably throw in some additional troops.

I find this puzzling in the wake of the recent leak of a highly classified message from Ambassador (and former General) Karl Eikenberry to the White House stating that additional troops should NOT be sent because of the corrupt state of the Afghan government. The message was something of a bombshell. Yet it was simply the latest message from the U.S. military to the effect that we should get out of Afghanistan. If one (correctly) reads between the lines, that was also the import of the famous McChrystal Report.

Eikenberry's message may have helped put an end to the President's seemingly endless indecision on the war. But, if he does announce that we will remain in Afghanistan (and perhaps send more troops), he would clearly be acting against the advice of the senior military officers in Afghanistan.

The President should by now have heard our in-country military - *which simply cannot say "Boss, we have got to get out of here"*- vote against continuing the war; as does the Ambassador in his brutally frank assessment. Instead, we see Secretary Clinton and General Jones, both of whom are obliged to support and follow the President's policies, putting heat on the Pakistanis to expand their fight with the Taliban, and on President Karzai in Afghanistan to reform his administration. Presumably in advance of the President's pending announcement.

The President has long since been told by our NATO allies that they will not increase their forces. The war goes increasingly badly for

U.S. in Afghanistan, and there is NO possibility that the incredible government corruption that both alienates the Afghan population and impedes progress in the war and "nation building" can be remedied. Building an Afghan Army to supplant U.S. forces is a wishful impossibility. Discussions on whether we should be fighting a counter-insurgency versus. a general war against all insurgents are fatuous. at best. It would appear that a "new strategy" means adopting a basically defensive posture against the insurgents: hold the major towns and cities and largely abandon the countryside to the insurgents.

It is clear that the Administration is NOT considering an aggressive war that would require at least 300,000 American soldiers and many billions of dollars of economic assistance over many years: a strategy that might stand a chance of creating a "democratic and pacified" Afghanistan. Nor is it plausible that Congress or the American people would support such a plan. Further, it is a fairly safe bet that the continuation of the war - with or without additional troops - would probably receive Congressional support (assuming continued Democratic Party dominance) for no more than a year or two. In my view it is completely implausible that we could turn Afghanistan around in that year or two, and that all the human and monetary resources expended in the period would be wasted.

If "holding the line" while the Afghan government "reforms" and a "new" Afghan Army is created is the President's goal, this will be a futile and costly exercise which, after a few years, will fail.

If, however, a Presidential decision to "hang in" - perhaps with some additional troops to help around the margins - *is the first step in a plan to begin negotiations with the Taliban and other insurgent groups intended to provide a sensible and face-saving means for U.S. to withdraw,* I believe the President has arrived at a correct and sensible plan of action. Carrying this thought further, such negotiations, carried on while we have substantial armed forces in-country, would hopefully lead to Taliban participation in a national jirga (assembly) to draw up a new constitution, followed by voting to establish a new government. And our exit.

Exit no matter how unstable the situation might be. We are NOT responsible for creating a happy, democratic and economically viable Afghanistan.

Pakistan, where the Taliban and domestic religious. crazies have stepped up the frequency and effectiveness of their attacks is an equally important issue. Our relations with that country worsen by the day: no Pakistan Army general or politician believes the U.S. will remain a reliable ally for years to come, and polls show that a majority of the Pakistani population believes that the U.S. is a greater enemy than the Taliban. The longer we remain in Afghanistan the more pressure Pakistan receives from both the Taliban and domestic religious. radicals calling for the destruction of the existing system of government.

If the President adopts the "hold the line" policy both the internal threat posed to Pakistan and our relations with that country will worsen.

If, however, the President embarks on the "negotiating from strength" policy, AND takes the Pakistanis into his confidence as *partners before and during the effort to execute the plan*, we will come out ahead on both counts.

I fervently hope that my speculation is on target.

Saturday, December 26, 2009

Obama's War

I admit that the President's recent decision to continue and radically expand the war in Afghanistan, while not unexpected, really knocked me off my perch. It has taken me several weeks of thought to test and try to deal fairly with his decision, hoping that I could find some merit, some valid justification, for Mr. Obama's new declaration of war. I have not.

No realistic evaluation of the facts surrounding the war supports his decision. I therefore conclude that Mr. Obama's decision was either a political one intended to foster his credibility as an able defender of American national security, or an egregious. error.

It was a monumentally wrong decision that will result, I believe, over the next year or two in the loss of many American lives and the expenditure of vast sums of money we do not have. After which we will leave Afghanistan having accomplished nothing except the relocation of various. elements of al-Qaeda and having significantly contributed to the destabilization of Pakistan.

Assuming Congress provides the funding, we will fairly soon have about 100,000 troops (plus about 100,000 "contractors" of various nationalities) in country to wage a guerrilla war against both *Taliban and non-Taliban fighters.* Unless Congress or public protest forces Mr. Obama to end the war, it will, as Secretary of Defense Robert Gates was honest enough to announce after the President's West Point speech, last years longer than Mr. Obama's utterly disingenuous (and purely politically motivated) assertion that our withdrawal "will begin" 18 months from now.

The decision was wrong because:

A) NO competent intelligence assessment of the situation supports the President's assertion that the war is "necessary" to "defeat" al-Qaeda;

B) By choosing to continue to fight Taliban and other insurgents with only enough additional troops (according to General McChrystal) to arrest our slide to defeat is, by definition, inadequate to "win."

Further, the President's decision NOT to engage in massive and wildly expensive "nation-building" in Afghanistan will deny the absolutely necessary economic adjunct to our military efforts to "pacify" the country. The President has willed a situation where there are neither enough combat troops to defeat the Taliban, nor enough economic assistance to fill-in behind the troops – a mandatory effort if gains paid for in blood are to be maintained.

C) It appears that the Administration's goal has shifted from trying to defeat the Taliban to ensuring that the insurgents can no longer threaten the Afghan Government's survival.

Hence, McChrystal's announced intention to focus on defending Kabul and other major population centers. Subsequent official statements, however, indicate that U.S. troops will seek out and fight the Taliban in the border areas with Pakistan. The goals, therefore, appear to be to "hold the cities" to demonstrate that the current Afghan Government is alive and well, while at the same time fighting to defeat the insurgents.

Note: we are seeing the first signs of serious splits between the White House and the military over what must be done in Afghanistan. This divergence is, I think, a revealing display of the President's vaguely "half-pregnant" view of the war and the realities the military faces on the ground.

If keeping the Afghan Government "alive and in operation" in Kabul and other major cities is Mr. Obama's goal and grand measure of success, we will certainly succeed: we can and will "hold" the major cities, which are and will continue to be infested with the enemy. And achieve nothing repeat nothing else. This is exactly the position the Soviets found themselves in in the years leading up to their withdrawal from Afghanistan. Hence this is an absolutely meaningless goal or measure of success.

D)   Mr. Obama's statement that his plan - even with the much longer timetable that Gates admits to - will give the U.S. time to raise, train and equip effective National Army and Police forces which will take over from us is at best willful self-deception.

No repeat no competent observer of the true present state of the pitiful so-called Afghan Army and Police, and their prospects over the next three or four years, believe that this is possible. Even if it were, that Army and Police would not be loyal to the Kabul Government, and, like their Soviet predecessors, will defect to the insurgent cause, or just go home.

E)   NATO (except for the Brits, who believe they have to pay for their "Special Relationship" with us) has utterly rejected the President's justification for the new war, and has refused to provide meaningful assistance. They are not being bloody minded - they can see the writing on the wall. Mr. Obama chooses to ignore this, as he clearly believes that even the token presence of handfuls of NATO troops makes it appear that the war is a NATO effort rather than the American war that it is.

F)   Pakistan will pay the immediate and too costly price for Obama's War. Our forces will no doubt push the Taliban and other insurgents back into Pakistan, where they will increase their already significantly expanded attacks on the Pak Government. This coupled with very serious domestic challenges to the Government by Pakistan's homegrown Islamic radicals, will threaten the already weak fabric of Pak governance and society.

G)   Pakistan itself is both unwilling and unable to fight a war against the insurgents at anything near the level that we have demanded. Further, since the Paks perceive we will NOT win in Afghanistan, and believe (as does the Taliban) that we have already announced that we will leave sooner rather than later, the Paks are rapidly losing their interest in fighting a war as American surrogates. (Witness news reports of increased Pak Military and Government harassment of official Americans in Pakistan. Strong signals that they are getting fed up with "our" war and "arrogant" Americans in general.)

It is sheer folly to believe that the Pak Army will respond positively to continued U.S. pressure to more vigorously engage the Taliban. Our assertion that it is in Pakistan's own long-term interest to escalate the fight with the Taliban/al-Qaeda is increasingly rejected by the Army and senior levels of the civilian government. The Paks, in fact, believe that the U.S. is the principal cause of their terrorist problems, which they see are the result of our driving the Taliban into Pakistan. Further, the more aggressive the U.S. is in Afghanistan, the more dangerous the Taliban threat becomes to Pakistan.

Thus goes this line of thinking, cutting a deal with the Taliban, which gives them sanctuary in the Frontier in return for ending their attacks in Pakistan is increasingly seen as the best way to serve Pakistan's long term interests.

I believe that the Paks will soon begin to curtail significantly our Pakistan-based activities, perhaps including restrictions on our absolutely indispensable supply route from Karachi to Afghanistan. And they will expand serious clandestine negotiations with the Taliban against the day of our departure in the relatively near future. After all, the Paks have to live with whatever is left in Afghanistan after we leave, and the most likely "power" they will have to deal with is the Taliban.

If the Pak Army's recent "all-out" incursion into South Waziristan is the best they can - or are willing - to do, the Army is not going to defeat the Taliban in the Frontier. That "big invasion" came after more than three months of warnings to the insurgents to get the hell out, and thus avoid a fight. That, and the Army's unverified claim to have killed only 600 out of the 12,000 insurgents the Paks said were there hardly suggests any real success or will to fight.

H)   Cost: In the 2009 Fiscal Year Congress appropriated $137 Billion for the war. Obama's War will significantly increase that cost - probably taking the price for each of the next two fiscal years close to $200 Billion.

The United States Treasury does not have a single dollar to cover this expenditure. Not one dollar. Every cent will have to be borrowed - along with all the many other billions of dollars that have to be borrowed to fund the exploding Federal deficit.

Which leads me to suggest one possible remedy: since Congress appears willing to fund this "down a rat hole" expenditure, should we (i.e., "the people") demand that Congress impose a "war tax" on all

Americans to pay for the war? I think that such a tax would be very unpopular, and, by focusing the public's mind on the war, would lead to demands that Congress NOT fund it. If it did not have that result, at least it would make this a pay-as-you-go enterprise instead of adding to an already disastrous deficit.

I)   Having made the belated discovery - largely in the wake of the recent Afghan elections - that Afghanistan is a cesspool of corruption at every level, Mr. Obama has demanded that President Karzai give immediate priority to a complete purge of the national and provincial governments, the justice system and the national police. Such reforms are correctly seen by the Administration as being absolutely crucial to the process of creating public support for the Government - which at the moment is nonexistent. Recognizing the need for these reforms does not mean that they will be made. In fact, they will not. The extent of corruption and the complications of tribal and ethnic claims make a mockery of the President's demands. There is no way that even modest improvements in these areas can be made in less than decades of hard work, much less than in the next several years. It is simply not possible.

J)   Finally, the Administration has apparently chosen not to face - or at least not to give proper weight to - the many realities that give the Taliban the upper hand in what amounts to a war to decide who controls the country. It is true that many, perhaps most, of the country's peasantry do not like the Taliban. That said, unbridled force rules: the Taliban's clear willingness to use the most brutal violence to control and intimidate the population is, regrettably, a highly effective method to master the countryside. Justified fear of Taliban atrocities forces compliance and denies us the ability to co-opt the population.

The Afghan population and the Taliban believe, with every justification, that the Americans are determined to leave Afghanistan, sooner rather than later. That fact alone makes the task established by the President impossible. My "First Law of the Third World" is that the inhabitants of a desperately divided and violent country want, more than anything else, to maximize their chances for survival by being on the" winning side" when the fighting is over. We are not perceived to be that side.

Whatever the reasoning behind Mr. Obama's decision to vastly expand the war, if any aspect of the war is "tested" by the application of hard facts - and the experience of our eight years of fighting in that country - his decision is seen to be wrong.

The sad fact, however, is that a Democratic Party-led Congress which fought so hard against "George Bush's Wars" is apparently, in the interest of party discipline in support of "their" President, prepared to borrow the money and spill the soldier blood needed to fight it.

The Republicans in Congress are no better: ignorance and/or spitefulness has them supporting Mr. Obama's War.

And "the country"- good Americans all - will presumably go along with the war.

Why?

First, since ours is a volunteer (as opposed to a conscript) military, the general population feels the personal pain of the war far less than, for example, in World War II, Korea and Vietnam, when the Draft touched everyone. Sadly, the all-volunteer military has produced a situation where most Americans now perceive a "military caste" that in some strange way seems detached from the body politic. "They" chose to be in the military, and since "they" are much less part of "U.S.," Presidents (and Congress) are much less inhibited in using "them." This is wrong.

Second, I suspect that most Americans assume that sensible and thoughtful people in Washington are usually right when it comes to spending the country's blood and treasure. In this instance, they are wrong.

In closing, I am sure that all who read this will join with me in wishing safe returns to the finest and most dedicated fighting men and women this country has ever sent to war.

This old snatch of poetry is surely theirs to claim:
"Ours is not to question why,
Ours is but to do or die."

Sunday, December 27, 2009

Iran: Is Revolution Possible?

Today, 27 December, is Ashura, the holiest day in the Shia Muslim calendar. As I write this crowds in Tehran (and other Iranian cities) are using the occasion to demonstrate against the clerical dictatorship. Every man and woman in these demonstrations knows that he or she is courting the certainty of beatings - and perhaps death - by participating. Yet, as they have for months, Iranians are choosing the only way they can to resist an evil regime operating in the best traditions of Nazi Germany.

The fact that these demonstrations have continued for months in the teeth of clerical-supported brutality clearly shows that the dissent that followed in the wake of President Ahmadinejad's stolen election was not a one-shot affair. In fact, my sense is that the current regime is in far greater trouble than it believed it would be last summer, and is in fact fighting for its life.

Over the past months, the regime has stepped up pressure on the opposition by introducing a number of measures that demonstrate the state's control and are intended to deter any active opposition. This has meant an expansion of restrictions on the freedoms and behavior of urban Iranians, and as intended, provides daily reminders of the looming threat of violent retribution against anyone daring to challenge the regime.

I increasingly have the sense that there are many similarities between the present circumstances and events in 1978, when the anti-Shah movement gathered strength and eventually prevailed. In early 1978 it seemed impossible that the Shah could be overthrown, but the opposition movement was steadily growing and expelled the Shah at the end of that year.

The months since the June 2009 election strike me as resembling the time from summer to fall of the Shah's last year in power. Few people would have believed in June of this year that the opposition movement would continue to roll on. This regime now stays in power only because it's Gestapo and SS (meaning the Basij and its masters, the Revolutionary Guard) are and have been using sufficient force to tamp down a full-scale revolution. There is an eerie similarity to the ultimate victory of anti-Shah forces after many months of apparently successful moves by the Shah to head off the opposition.

The Shah was overthrown in a remarkably brief period of time as a result of the rapid growth of the anti-Shah opposition. In the Shah's case, his tools of repression, particularly the Army, simply collapsed and refused to kill its own citizenry. His secret service was rendered ineffective when faced with overwhelming numbers of anti-Shah Iranians. His Imperial Guard briefly fought valiantly before it too collapsed either dead or refusing to fire on men, women, and children. Most Iranians, even if they are too young to remember or participate in the revolution 30 years ago, are well aware of the speed with which an apparently unassailable government was overthrown. Perhaps history is repeating itself.

I now think it is fully possible that the current versions of the Shah's instruments of repression will also not be able to withstand a large-scale movement from below.

President Ahmadinejad has clearly come to represent the evils of the clerical dictatorship, and, at least in urban Iran, he is vilified. The survival of Ahmadinejad and the Supreme Leader, Ayatollah Ali Khamenei, are now inextricably linked. This helps the opposition since, as a tactical measure, it allows the opposition to focus on them as opposed to clerics in general as a target. We must remember that a significant number of Iran senior clergy are opposed to Ahmadinejad and the Supreme Leader, Ayatollah Ali Khamenei.

Much depends on what happens today in Iran. If the demonstrations are widespread and are met with widespread reprisals – beatings, shootings – the regime has moved one more step towards the end of its perilous existence - when the issue will really become whether the tools of repression can suppress the opposition or not.

The regime is on the horns of the kind of dilemma frequently faced by dictatorial regimes supported by brute power. Does continued violence and killing risk triggering an overwhelming national revolt? Additionally, the regime must consider whether enough members of the Revolutionary Guard and Basij are prepared to kill their demonstrating countrymen in order to maintain their dominance? On the other hand, is an essentially leaderless opposition prepared to die in sufficient numbers to stoke the fires of rebellion to a successful end?

Sunday, December 27, 2009

President Obama and Iran, Part I

Like Afghanistan and Iraq, Iran has long since "belonged" to Mr. Obama, whose policy towards Tehran has consisted of bending over backwards to be conciliatory to Iran's President Ahmadinejad and the religious dictatorship. That policy has now proven to be utterly bankrupt.

(**Note**: for an excellent review of U.S. policies towards Iran since President Obama took office see: the 27 December 2009 "Weekly Standard" article by Stephen Hayes titled, "2010: Regime Change in Iran.")

A new and more rational policy must now be devised: a policy that acknowledges that the President does not have mystical powers of persuasion; that recognizes that the present Iranian Government WILL continue its march towards the acquisition of nuclear weapons and more advanced weapons delivery systems if it is not forced to pay too high a price to do so; that the U.S. might have to act unilaterally to deal with Iran; and that Iran is in the midst of a profound internal crisis that both complicates and offers U.S. policy opportunities.

One can hope that Mr. Obama has learned a few lessons from the past year. Take the President's position towards the Iranian regime's bloody reprisals in the wake of the mass demonstrations against the clerical tyranny which broke out after massively fraudulent elections last June. Mr. Obama has studiously avoided making any meaningful gestures of sympathy or understanding towards the many Iranians who have risked beatings and death while standing up for their basic human and political rights.

Rights which Americans have traditionally supported.

Iranian protesters, perhaps echoing a handful of Bush-league Norwegian politicians who saw Mr. Obama to be some sort of vaguely messianic "great new world leader," chanted his name in the streets asking for some recognition from him of their plight and sacrifice. They got nothing in return, and now chant their condemnation of his refusal to condemn their oppressors. A few months ago it is likely that the most pro-American people around were those very protesters, who understandably looked to America for, at the least, moral support. No longer: Mr. Obama has deliberately compromised America's position on the high moral ground.

The President's apparent icy indifference was, one may safely assume, prompted by his belief that he, unlike his predecessor, could extend a warm hand of negotiation and arrive at some sort of deal with Iran over its nuclear weapons program. A deal was offered to Iran - and what a deal it was to have been. It would have relieved Iran from the threat of any sort of American reprisals, while actually assisting Iran's move forward with both its nuclear weapons and missile delivery systems program.

Fortunately for us, the offer was turned down by Tehran for domestic political reasons: anti-Ahmadinejad politicians accused him of giving away the store if he accepted it. Charges which, while untrue, apparently forced him to reject what would have been a highly advantageous agreement.

Friday, January 1, 2010

The New Model Afghan National Army: An Oxymoron

Readers will recall that I have made a number of negative references to the creation of an Afghan National Army, an entity that the President states will be created to replace U.S. troops in Afghanistan. In fact, Mr. Obama has basically justified our greatly expanded military presence there as being necessary to provide time to create this Army. It would be difficult to find a more fatuous reason to remain at war in that country.

I do not believe that anything approaching a credible military force supporting the Afghan Government can be created: certainly not in a period of less than a decade or more. We have, after all, already been working at this hopeless task for more than seven years.

Current plans call for creating an Army of about 170,000 by July 2011 - the putative start date for our withdrawal. Plans are for the Army to grow to about 240,000 by July 2014. Army strength today is nominally 90,000, but it is generally agreed that no more than 52,000 actually turn up for duty. The desertion rate is high, and the use of drugs while on duty is normal.

The realities of the country's tribal structure and loyalties; it's contentious ethnic and language divisions; the time-honored structure of war lord dominance; and the populations' utter contempt for the central government are obstacles too great to overcome. Afghan tribals do not make good soldiers: regimentation, discipline and plain old hard "soldier" work are utterly repugnant to them. They are brigands and great part-time guerrillas, but not good soldier material. The powerful Taliban steadily penetrates and manipulates the "new" Army, and the population from which the Army is drawn knows that the Americans will "soon" be leaving - abandoning the government and whatever passes for an Army. The task is simply beyond our abilities.

Thursday, January 7, 2010

Terrorism: Failed Defenses

THE "CHRISTMAS BOMBER"

Perhaps the old adage that "God takes care of drunks, little children, and the United States of America" worked on Christmas Day. Or we were just lucky.

We have not yet been told why the explosive device did not detonate. Was it that the Bomber messed up, or was the design of the "trigger" mechanism faulty and no detonation was actually possible?

Note: PETN (which the press reports was the explosive used by the Bomber), like all "high order" explosives (e.g., TNT and the family of "plastic" explosives), MUST have a small but powerful "high order" explosive go off in or on it to initiate detonation. This is normally a "blasting cap" detonator, ignited either electrically or by a burning fuse. The detonator provides the shock wave that instantly ignites/explodes the PETN. All "plastic explosives" are very "stable" - i.e., it takes a good deal of energy to set them off. You can fire a bullet into a block of wood and it will NOT detonate. You can cut a piece off the block, light it with a match and use it as a heat source under your fondue pot. Blasting caps are pretty much fool proof - but they are metallic, and hence can show up in metal detectors. So ... perhaps his bomb makers tried to avoid using one, and relied on some other means to provide the "shock" to set the PETN off.

Despite the Administration's mildly frenetic efforts immediately after the incident to assure us that the "system worked," it did not. Not by a mile. I was particularly offended by ex-CIA officer John Brennan, now thoroughly politicized and the White House's Counter-Terrorism "main man," saying that it did. Brennan was a long time CIA analyst (not a field operations officer) before he retired in 2005, and was Mr. Obama's "intelligence advisor" during the campaign. Never one of his admirers, I utterly reject both his assertions that the country is on top of the terrorism problem and that bringing terrorists to trial as common criminals is a fine idea.

It is interesting that the President, speaking to the country Tuesday afternoon, flatly contradicted Brennan's statements (and similar assertions by other Administration stalwarts like Secretary Napolitano) by his admission that the "system" had not worked.

Back to basics: I have seen no evidence that Mr. Obama has recognized - certainly not up to Christmas Day - that we really are at war with an evil and malicious enemy whose modus operandi violates all norms of civilized behavior, and that captured terrorists should be treated accordingly. This vaguely unreal attitude is shared by his senior White House advisors – Homeland Security Chief Janet Napolitano being the most invidious example.

I have for many months felt that his attitude towards the terrorist threat was detached and pro forma. He has refused to admit that the premeditated murder of 13 soldiers by a Muslim Army officer was an act of terrorism, in effect identifying it as a plain old mass murder.

To date the President has backed off from the aggressive stance adopted by former President Bush. Witness his orders NOT to refer to "The War on Terror" and to down-play the subject as a whole; his decision to prosecute CIA and other interrogators for using tools approved by a previous President and Justice Department to obtain precious information needed to save American and other lives; his questionable decision to honor his campaign promise to close Guantanamo and to try terrorists in Federal Courts as common criminals - along with the likes of Martha Stewart and Bernie Madoff. How long will the government be able to incarcerate terrorists who, by being placed in American jails, are thus entitled to all the rights and protections afforded by the Constitution? How many more terrorists will be released to their country of origin only to surface later as active terrorists working against us?

Perhaps Christmas Day will have been Mr. Obama's epiphany. Perhaps not. Perhaps, if he senses the gut anger of the American public against both terrorists and inadequate government commitment to fighting them, he may - for political reasons alone - become less distanced and more emotionally involved. An effective war against our fanatic Islamic enemies requires Presidential leadership that reflects iron resolve and true conviction that the President has not, thus far, shown the nation.

And the Christmas Day bomber? He started talking to the FBI until the lawyers got to him. Now silence.

The President's speech was candid in recognizing that there were huge systemic failures in our counter-terrorism structure. He has announced that these failures are to be identified, and corrective measures implemented. Since the same people who were in charge before Christmas Day are now in charge of identifying and fixing the very failures they denied existed prior to the President's speech, I have little confidence that much will be done.

The Blame Game

Mrs. Napolitano, the person most specifically charged with the defending the country against Muslim kamikazes, clearly heads the list. First, because her attitude towards terrorism clearly reflects what is to me an incomprehensible and willful determination to refuse to see terrorism for what it is. This is the woman who dislikes the word "terrorism" and prefers the term "man-caused disasters." Who specifically rejects acknowledging that large numbers "man-causing-disasters" have declared war against the nation - and refuses to state that we are in fact in a war against terrorism? With that philosophical bent, why should we expect aggressive, competent leadership? Second, her assertions in the wake of Christmas Day that the system had worked just fine tell me that she is either dumb or Totally Unaware. Whatever the cause, I think that she has clearly demonstrated that she is in the wrong job.

Next on my list is the Office of the Director of National Intelligence: an office created by the ill-considered recommendation of the 9/11 Commission. The premise for its establishment was that the DNI is to sit on the top of the pyramid of over twenty intelligence agencies and make sure there are NO gaps in intelligence collection/coverage/dissemination. Instead it has been built into a large organization replicating work done by other agencies; taking responsibilities from CIA, which it is not competent to address and has not attended to, and is generally confusing the issues. It clearly failed on Christmas Day. The fact that President Obama did not even mention the DNI in his speech demonstrates his and his agency's irrelevance.

My friends in the FBI assure me, I'm sorry to say, that their agency is in poor shape as regards the counter-terrorism issue.

A minor note: over one-half of the population of Gitmo, about 130 persons - has been "cleared for release." Many of this group were to go to Yemen, where many prisoners have already been sent. Mr. Obama just announced that no more will go there. He did not mention that he made this decision because so many of those previously "cleared" and exported to Yemen are back in the terrorist game. That fact has been known for many months: it took the Christmas Day bomber incident to lead the President to cut off what was an easy way for us to be rid of detainees -- and had become a detainee escape route back to terrorism.

All of the remaining detainees swear that they have never been terrorists (and, just in case they might have been, promise never to be again). Experience has proven that there is no country to which we can export them without the very high risk of their being released and returning to the jihad. So, per Attorney General Holder's idea, I assume they will be brought to the U.S., where they will be covered by the Constitutional rights of the country whose citizens they wish to destroy. Please ask your criminal lawyer friends if they think that these people can be detained, much less convicted; the detainees will allege having been tortured, "Miranda" will throw out confessions, etc., etc.

Afghanistan

Could there be more dramatic proof that al-Qaeda has long since abandoned Afghanistan as a haven/launch point than the information that has surfaced publicly since Christmas Day on how that organization is now based in Yemen, Somalia, etc.?

Will this fact now dawn on the Administration, and suggest that the President's recent assertion that we MUST remain in Afghanistan in order to defeat al-Qaeda might be invalid? And perhaps be reviewed?

I doubt it. But it should be.

Yemen

Having visited Yemen a number of times, and having watched developments there for over 35 years, it is perfectly clear to me why al-Qaeda has shifted much of its operational base to this disaster of a so-called country, where there are plenty of "man causing disasters." Now that the public spotlight is focused there, perhaps the Administration will give it some long overdue major attention.

But, pray God, not invade the place.

The CIA Base in Afghanistan

In the dangerous and complicated world of spies and counter spies the "double agent" is an ever-present threat. All agents ("spies" in the popular vernacular) are potential "double agents." All. Thus perhaps the first rule of "agent handling" is to take every possible measure to defend against that possibility. This fundamental rule was clearly not observed in the recent tragedy at a CIA Base in Afghanistan.

It grieves me to say this, but the deaths appear to be entirely the result of an utter lack of professionalism and disregard for the most basic rules of defensive security.

Which, I am equally sad to say, is the direct result of the mauling CIA has taken over the past years from a Democratic Congress, this and previous Presidents, and a vindictive former Vice President named Cheney. This has driven capable people out of the Agency, leaving it desperately short of experienced managers and mentors at every level – particularly in the Agency's Clandestine Service.

There is no better indicator of the Agency's malaise than the fact that over sixty percent of its work force has been on duty for three years or less; this in a business where it takes years of hands-on experience to learn a very difficult trade. The Agency's roles and responsibilities - particularly in the middle of several wars - have been so diced up, confused and restricted that there is no chance that it could be reconstituted for years (even if the President wanted that to happen.) It is amazing it is still getting anything done at all. And it is.

Thursday, January 21, 2010

President Obama and Iran, Part II

Introductory Comment: The following assessments and conclusions are made on the basis of my rigorous review of what is available in the media, and from my experience in 1976-79, when I was a very close witness to the revolution that expelled the Shah and installed the current regime. My thesis is an objective one: In truth I am not an admirer of the country writ large, and have found Iranians to be a difficult, emotional, and troubled people with a long history of acquiescence to dictatorial rule. There is certainly no tradition of democratic government in Iran. Down deep, however, a great many Iranians have come to share American concepts of individual freedom - which is why I place so much stress on the importance of moral support when they are struggling, unaided, for those liberties.

A nuclear-armed Iran, we all agree, would be a nightmare. It is now more than proven that there is no repeat no possibility that this or any other Administration can talk clerical Iran out of its pursuit of "the bomb." Nor will the world community agree to impose the harsh sanctions that might, and I stress the word "might," deter the regime from its nuclear weapons program. A revolution overthrowing the clerical tyranny would serve American - and many other - interests because it is much more likely that a "new Iran" could be cajoled not to pursue nuclear power status. And, of course, a revolution might result in creating a nation with meaningful personal liberties - not a bad thing, actually.

A minor aside: in the "old days" CIA would no doubt have long since been directed by a President to try to provide the sort of assistance that, at the margins, might enable this revolution to "happen." By, for example, helping dissidents sort-out who is and is not trustworthy; identifying operatives; and establishing secure communications networks.

No more: Iranians are on their own and for the moment the clerics and their thugs hold the upper hand.

In late December 2009 I wrote a piece titled "President Obama and Iran, Part I" , the main point of which was that the President's year-long policy of negotiating with Iran over its nuclear weapons program has failed utterly. In that year Iran has continued to build its stock of enriched nuclear material, to develop advanced missile delivery systems, and to harden their nuclear installations against attack.

Further, I criticized Mr. Obama for his icy determination virtually to ignore the violent suppression of the huge anti-clerical protest movement in Iran.

My purpose here is to draw your attention to what I believe are the very grave consequences of Mr. Obama's refusal to provide moral support to the Iranian opposition, and to explain why American moral support is unusually and uniquely important in the Iranian context.

I believe that a vast majority of Iranians, particularly the large well-educated population, want to be rid of a ghastly dictatorship that remains in power only by using violent repressive measures. Faced by this shameless tyranny, the exact equivalent of that seen in Hitler's Germany and Stalin's Russia, the populace has only one weapon: the massive displays of outrage and rebellion they have mounted since June of 2009. Continued "mass action" depends entirely on the opposition's continued courage and will power, which, to a very large degree, depend on moral support from the world - particularly from the United States.

The only way that Iran's clerical despotism can be overthrown is from within, which means that large numbers of Iranians - in the teeth of violent repression - must continue large-scale anti-regime demonstrations. They must also plan and organize demonstrations and other actions against the clerical government. Then, I submit, just as happened in the 1978-79 revolution against the Shah, the momentum of the national demand for freedom will at some point overwhelm the ruling minority.

The nascent Iranian revolution - which I think eventually will be successful - has several enormous handicaps. The first of which is that there is no recognized leader around whom the opposition might coalesce. There is no figurehead, no focus, and no "flag" around which the opposition can rally. History shows that most revolutions require a figurehead. The Shah's collapse in 1978-79 proves the point: the Ayatollah Khomeini provided exactly the dynamic focus that revolution required.

The two opposition leaders who surfaced after the June 2009 elections, while certainly willing to stick their necks out, are men of insufficient character, courage, or dynamism to provide this catalyst. Iranians know that, but their need for some central players around whom they might rally has forced them to make use of the best they have: weak men, not up to the moment. Unfortunately, baring the semi-miraculous appearance of some as-yet-unknown "Man on a White Horse," this situation will continue. This means the opposition must make do with some form of psychological mass "consensus," which can only be created and sustained by a shared sense of doing the right and noble thing - and for that, external encouragement must be provided.

The second enormous impediment faced by the essentially leaderless opposition is the regime's willingness to resort to brutality on the streets, and to wage a campaign of illegal arrest, detention and torture of the more active and articulate supporters of the opposition movement. So far, when faced by street crowds, the regime has been able to maintain the fine balance between using "enough" force and outright butchery. The regime knows its people, and is well tuned to how much and what kind of violence is needed in a given situation, particularly when dealing with street demonstrations.

More important, the government has chosen to exercise on the deadly and effective technique of midnight arrests, illegal detention, and hidden torture to eviscerate the opposition movement by quietly "cutting out" its most dangerous opponents. The regime carefully makes it known that it never acts against only one person in a family or a larger association of individuals. An arrest, a "disappearance," torture, a beating, a job loss; a death - all those associated with a victim are aware that they too are "known," and are potentially subject to similar treatment. Each single act of silent violence creates a circle of people who know that they are on a list ... and are already guilty by association.

It is difficult for Americans to understand how brutally effective these tactics are, and how well they serve the regime by creating an all-embracing environment of fear of the midnight knock on the door. And of distrust, since this system of management-by-terror depends on having a mass of informants, of which there are many: informants created, as often as not, by actual or threatened torture. By establishing a pervasive climate of fear and fostering distrust in the ranks of the people, the regime has so far kept the upper hand.

The extent of this silent, invisible program of threat, jail, and death is far more widespread than has been - or can be, given the threat of reprisals - reported in the West. For a people who want only their most basic human rights, Iran is well into a night of terror.

Yet ... there is no meaningful international condemnation - least of all by the United States - of this barbarous state of affairs. Our President and Europe operate as though Iran is a civilized country.

In addition, the regime's ability to disrupt internal communications, and to shut down news to and from the outside world, is a tremendous handicap to the process of organizing and maintaining an effective opposition movement. This is one of the principle differences between the 1979 revolution and today. The Shah did not try to cut Iran off from the world, and in fact Khomeini's supporters successfully manipulated the Western press, using it to arrange mass protests and broadcast anti-Shah disinformation.

A third problem is that the sizeable Iranian Diaspora, which almost by definition is anti-clerical, does not appear to be providing support to their friends on the streets in Iran. I have seen no reporting that indicates that "overseas" Iranians - mostly in Britain, the U.S. and France - are doing much to help. Specifically, there is no evidence that these "exiles," unlike their predecessors in 1979, are organizing, assisting and fostering the opposition in Iran. This does not surprise me: Iranians very much tend to avoid individual acts of defiance - they prefer to work in herds. Another reason is the fact that the Iranian secret service, operating with impunity in this country and in Europe, has penetrated virtually all groups of potential activists. Their primary task is to make it clear that anti-regime activity abroad by individuals or groups will result in serious harm to relatives remaining in Iran. Thus the Iranian Gestapo here in the U.S. and Europe has driven many potential supporters to ground. And, again, there is no figurehead around which anti-regime elements can gather.

The final missing ingredient in this proto-revolutionary stage in Iran is moral support from the only country that matters (in the minds of Iranians): the United States.

Most Iranians know full well that the regime's 30-year long anti-American diatribe is a tactic often adopted by dictatorships: every tyranny needs a "foreign devil" to blame for its failures and to justify internal repression. The regime's endless anti-U.S. rhetoric, in the mind of all but the poorest and most rural Iranians, is recognized for what it is. In no way does that noise reflect the view most Iranians hold of America.

Iran's relationship to the United States is an unusual one. Virtually every Iranian would above all things treasure the right to live in the United States, and American ideals and individual liberties have enormous significance in the Iranian psyche. It is vastly more important to Iranians, for example, that an American President condemn the suppression of their legitimate human rights than similar words by a French President or a British Prime Minister.

This affinity for America and things American was what struck me most during my three years in Iran (before and after the Shah's fall.) I have lived and worked in a fair number of countries, and I have never witnessed the extraordinary and deeply felt associations so many Iranians have for "the States." All else aside, most Iranians look at the United States as THE symbol of freedom; THE system they admire and wish to emulate; and, ultimately, THE source of encouragement in their dark days.

It is not an overstatement to say that the survival and eventual success of Iran's legitimate opposition movement, faced by the grave impediments noted above, in many ways depends on clearly articulated support by an American President, and by his instructing his foreign affairs agencies and our UN Mission to follow his lead. The theme is simply that of illuminating the Iranian regime's criminal suppression of the basic human rights of its people, and criticizing its violation of every tenet of the United Nations Charter. He should also take the lead in the international arena, calling on the world to take notice and condemn the evil happenings in Iran.

I believe that Mr. Obama's apparent indifference to the plight of Iran's demonstrators has played a major role in assisting the clerical despotism to suppress what they clearly recognize is a very real threat to their continued existence.

I fully realize the care with which statements of support for Iran's opposition movement must be framed. In Iran's case, however, about the only rule that must be followed is not repeat not to call for violent insurrection or to promise armed support for the opposition. As the recent past has proven, even Mr. Obama's faint expressions of condemnation of the regime have drawn immediate and vitriolic criticism from Mr. Ahmadinejad and his masters. What more could the regime say in response to meaningful expressions of moral support than it has already said to mild criticisms? The regime's real response is measured by its continued determination to become a nuclear threat.

Since Iran's rejection of the West's latest and very generous offer on the nuclear issue, it appears from the press that Mr. Obama has learned that he cannot talk the regime out of its nuclear weapons program: the President has issued instructions to identify additional sanctions that might be imposed on Iran.

Unfortunately, sanctions are NOT a credible means to deter Iran from its present course. I wrote some months ago that sanctions - which to be effective would have to be implemented by the U.S., the EU, Russia, China and Japan - will not dissuade Iran from the nuclear path. The only exception to this might be if an effective embargo on Iran's imports of automobile and truck fuels was put in place. Russia has already made clear that it will not support this specific sanction. The Chinese have stated that they will not support any sanctions, and Japan is not likely to agree to the expansion of existing sanctions.

Thus any additional sanctions the Administration might cook up, even if they were supported by the European Union, will fail. This means that Mr. Obama, sooner or later, must face the decision whether to use military force to delay or destroy Iran's growing nuclear weapons capability.

Given the President's long agony over the war in Afghanistan, it seems very doubtful that he would be willing to declare war on Iran. Further, given the effort Iran has made to disperse and bury its nuclear facilities, there are very serious reasons to question whether U.S. air attacks would be successful at inflicting really serious damage. (Note: for a recent update on the difficulties related to military action, please see a 5 January 2010 New York Times article "Iran Shielding Its Nuclear Efforts in a Maze of Tunnels.") There are, in fact, a good many valid reasons for the U.S. NOT to attack Iran.

Israel, of course, is the wild card regarding the use of force. It strikes me that it is very unlikely that Israel would attempt, on its own, to strike Iranian nuclear facilities: despite Israeli bravura, it simply does not have adequate means to do so.

It is possible, however, that the Israelis might launch their own attacks, particularly if they believe that President Obama will not use military force. If they do chose to attack, Israel fully realizes that Iran will and can strike back effectively- both directly and by employing the very strong Hezbollah and Hamas forces it has armed so well. (In their most recent encounter, Hezbollah's missiles - now greatly augmented by Iran in numbers and effectiveness - very nearly won the day.)

I suspect that the Israelis would only do this if they believed that a highly effective Iranian/Hezbollah response would force the Americans into a war with Iran. If that response was sufficiently effective that it raised the issue of Israel's survival, I am quite sure the Israelis are right.

All of which, I believe, argues for the President to mount a long-term strategy of condemning the present Iranian government and expressing sympathy and support for Iran's oppressed people.

Thursday, January 28, 2010

Terrorism and the Obama Response

The policies and procedures adopted by this Administration to deal with Islamic terrorism have moved from being unwise and uncomprehending to policies that deliberately place the United States at great risk. I will review some of these policies below, and explain why I believe they pose a very real - and unnecessary - danger to our country.

The first and most critical requirement in our national response to terrorism is a President's understanding of the unusual nature of the threat, and his attitude and commitment to fighting it. This cannot be overstated, since a President's fundamental commitment - or lack thereof - drives every aspect of our counter-terrorism effort. Mr. Obama has shifted from George Bush's very vocal, hard-nosed, and pragmatic approach to a policy of soft-pedaling the issue, while at the same time restricting our ability to fight back by introducing strict politically correct legal parameters to all aspects of our response to the terrorist challenge. I believe Mr. Obama has failed the country miserably by vitiating a necessarily unorthodox response to an unorthodox enemy. I have struggled to try to understand his thinking in formulating his approach and policies: testing them against what I know about the subject after a lifetime of dealing with Islam and Islamic terrorism on a professional basis. I cannot find satisfactory real-world explanations for them. I do not know if the President's actions/policies are the consequence of a naive refusal to understand the nature and extent of the terrorist threat; or sheer narcissism (the "over-evaluation of one's own attributes or achievements".) I am dead certain, however, that if the worst of these policies are not reversed the country will see more terrorism and more successful terrorist acts directed against us.

I have no sense that Mr. Obama feels any emotional antipathy towards terrorists and terrorism. Nor do I feel he has deep-seated, instinctive "I am an American and I will defend America against its enemies" convictions. I do not expect theatre, and I guess I can live with his frequently icy and dispassionate delivery style, but I do expect him to display - which in my view he does not - a very public total, unquestioned commitment to the defense of this country. I also expect him to adopt policies that at least give us a fighting chance to counter successfully the barbaric actions of our Islamic terrorist enemies.

So, apparently, does the public. A Pell survey of the public's top priorities released on 25 January 2010 has the economy, jobs, and terrorism bunched together at the top of a list of 21 items {83-80 percent, respectively}. Health care came in at 49; global warming at 28. The terrorist ranking is essentially the same as one year ago: the entire period of his stewardship.

The next item in my catalog of the President's missteps is his clear determination not to acknowledge that America is at war with terrorists. Today more Americans have died in the U.S. as a result of terrorist attacks than were killed at Pearl Harbor. Our enemy says that it is at war with us. He, however, and thus his Administration, have bent over backwards to avoid acknowledging that we are at war, refusing to use the Bush Administration's clear and unequivocal assertions that we are in a War on Terror. Why does the President deny what the American public - and the world - knows very well? Is it not more than a little cynical to send troops to die in something other than a war?

Note: the one exception to this is Afghanistan, where for what I believe to be political reasons (to demonstrate his anti-terrorist credentials) he has increased our military commitment to "defeat al-Qaeda:" a huge, unaffordable, unwinnable, unnecessary, and unwarranted war. I consider that war to be the most egregious of his "counter-terrorist" actions. Recent statements by several of the most important players in that war - the U.S. Ambassador to Afghanistan and General Petraeus, the theater commander - are clearly intended to inform the President that even with almost doubling our military effort the war is a losing proposition. (**Note**: I will discuss those statements in a separate piece.)

Next on the list are his decisions to close Guantanamo (which played well with the American Left and very well indeed with his leftist European "constituency,") and to try terrorists in U.S. Federal courts as common criminals with all the Constitutional protections and guarantees given American citizens.

Guantanamo was established by the Bush Administration for several reasons: it physically isolated terrorists from American communities; and it purposely enabled the Government to keep captured terrorists (who are, to repeat, not legitimate enemy combatants but rather are killers operating outside all recognized international rules of conduct) from access to American criminal defense procedures. Gitmo was abolished specifically to allow these killers access to U.S. courts. Or to force their release, which has resulted in many known cases of terrorists returning to the war. This to me is placing obsessive political correctness before the national welfare. The negative ramifications of this decision are simply dreadful. To name a few: the media circus attending the trials will serve to publicize and benefit the terrorist cause. They will not, as the President says, illustrate our "fairness," but rather, in the eyes of the Muslim world, will define our weakness. The trials may very well result in failing to obtain convictions and result in the mandated release of many terrorists. And they provide a golden opportunity for terrorists to stage attacks in the U.S.: attacks which from their point of view will serve to demonstrate their strength.

Mr. Obama's obsessively politically correct policies regarding the treatment of captured terrorists are absurd: witness his insistence that terrorists (for example, the "Underwear Bomber") are presumed to be innocent and are to be given all the legal rights available under American criminal jurisprudence. And they are dangerous, in that they bring the very real threat of terrorist attacks on the communities where such trials are to be held. (Add to this the cost of providing security for the trials: the bill for the handful of trials scheduled for New York is $200 million.) The most odious and important adverse consequence of Mr. Obama's shift to the application of leftist law school rules for dealing with terrorists is that they effectively restrict the pursuit of intelligence. No real defense against Islamic terrorism is possible without the aggressive pursuit of information, and the introduction of "Miranda rules" has tied our hands.

I quote former Navy Secretary John Lehman's recent article on "How Obama Is Blowing the War on Terror." QUOTE: It is now official Obama policy that for {terrorist} information in the intelligence bureaucracy to be acted upon (for instance, putting someone on a watch list because of a warning from that person's father that he might be a terrorist) such information must first meet the legal evidentiary standard set in the Supreme Court case Terry v. Ohio, To wit: "Reasonable suspicion requires "articulable" facts which ...

warrant a determination that an individual is .. or has been engaged in ... terrorist activities. UNQUOTE

Think on that: under that rule it could easily be argued that there would have been no reason to place "Underwear Man" on a Watch List. Is this a decision some low- or mid-level person in the bureaucracy is to make, a hundred times a day, without a lawyer on hand? With Big Brother looking over his or her shoulder to ensure that in doubtful cases (which always make up the bulk of "raw" information) the analyst must now err on the side of the individual. Please.

All of this against the background of Attorney General Holder bringing criminal actions against CIA personnel conducting interrogations under the Bush Administration's ground rules; and the court martial of three Navy SEALs for punching the killer of four Americans in Iraq.

Next, I utterly condemn Mr. Obama's absolute prohibition against placing captured terrorists in any situation which the ACLU would define as "torture." That order, coupled with "Miranda," has virtually destroyed our ability to collect vital intelligence from terrorists who have information we must have to defend an innocent society. Without that precious human intelligence we are lost. (I have written previously on the subject of "torture," and the reader might wish to dig that article up from my Blog. I wish to stress that the "torture" Mr. Obama has forbidden is in fact the perception of physical harm, not actual physical harm. And this technique was approved by the Department of Justice and was briefed to Congress and approved.)

All of us find real torture repugnant and oppose it. I have really been tortured and I am particularly against it. But I urge the reader, no matter how viscerally against water boarding, to thoughtfully examine the very high stakes in the counter-terror war, the nature of the technique involved, and the background of those who were (or could be) subject to the technique. I believe that when one weighs all of these considerations the use of water boarding on a selective basis (as was the case in selecting a total of twelve "high-value" terrorist captives) is necessary, justifiable, and within the bounds of conscience. Let us remember the extraordinary nature of the threat; the fact that almost all victims of terrorist barbarity are (as they are intended to be) innocents, and the desperate need for human intelligence.

Perhaps it would be a worthwhile exercise to "war game" the issue. Suppose "Underwear Man" had been successful and hundreds of innocents had been murdered. Then suppose that the post-attack study revealed that we had had several new Yemen-based known terrorist captives whom we realistically could assume had knowledge of various attack plans - but had refused to divulge any information about anything. Would not most of us believe - particularly after the above became public knowledge - that it would have been worth bending our inherent distaste for water boarding to try to obtain information sufficient to head-off the disaster? When I reflect deeply on this very real world situation I would vote for water boarding.

That situation exists today, just as I write these words.

Aside from denying us vital information that can only be obtained from human sources, this injunction has two adverse side effects: it forces our human intelligence collectors to take risks that are far beyond the "acceptable" while trying to make up for the loss of this gold mine of information; and it gives all terrorists the sure and comfortable knowledge that the worst that can happen to them if they are captured is that they will be read their Miranda rights.

I also object to the President's refusal to call the terrorism we face "Islamic terrorism." That is what it is, and what it has been for many years. No one in the Arab or other world thinks otherwise. No purpose is served by willfully ignoring where the terrorists who attack us come from, and the fact that they claim that Islam both rewards and legitimizes their activities. He apparently found it necessary to apologize to the Arab and Muslim world for America's alleged abuse of its power for many decades. To refuse to acknowledge from where and why our enemies come defies logic. More importantly, it relieves the Islamic world of any sense of responsibility for being the source of this horror, thus depriving U.S. vital support from non-radicalized Muslims. That world must speak out more than it has to condemn the use of terror, and to refute the use of Islam to legitimize and justify terrorism - particularly the suicide bomber. "Normal" and "civilized" Islam must take the lead in refuting the entire concept that violence, particularly terrorist violence, is "okay."

This obfuscation, coupled with the new restrictions imposed by "Miranda" rules, his Muslim antecedents, and his decision - as an adult - to change his name to conform to Muslim practice, has left him open to criticism for being a Muslim "sympathizer." True or not, it seems to me this would hardly be an advantage at the polls, to say nothing of when trying to lead the American people against Muslim-based terrorism.

The President's limited reference to counter-terrorism in his State of the Union speech claimed substantial progress under his Administration. I will guarantee that very few people actually involved in that war (and I note that he did not use the "war" word) would agree with his assertions. His claim that more al-Qaeda types were killed or captured in 2009 is true. However, in the main those successes were achieved as a result of the previous Administration's policies: under the President's new rules the news a year from now will be very different indeed.

A final thought: I submit that every terrorist in the world applauds Mr. Obama's election and his new policies.

Could there be a more devastating commentary?

Wednesday, February 3, 2010

The President and Iran - Addendum

On 21 January 2010 I wrote an article on this blog that criticized President Obama's handling of the Iranian situation. In that piece I focused on the complete failure of Mr. Obama's policy of attempting to negotiate with Tehran on the nuclear weapons issue, and criticized him for not providing moral support for the nascent Iranian revolution against the country's repressive regime: support which I believe is particularly important in the Iranian context.

For the moment that regime clearly feels it has the upper hand. To demonstrate that it has suppressed the popular uprising, and to lay down another warning card against the resumption of opposition activities, the clerical regime has begun executing dissidents arrested in the wake of the post-election protests. Two dissidents were recently hung, and at least five more are said to be awaiting the noose.

We have no idea how many hundreds of dissidents remain in jail, or how many more will be executed. And the regime's silent Gestapo-like campaign to identify and silence dissidents continues unabated.

This as punishment for demonstrating for their most basic human rights.

Once again, Mr. Obama has chosen to look the other way. The only criticism of this immoral behavior to come from the White House was a brief statement by Deputy Press Secretary Bill Burton, who managed to say that "We see it as a low point in the Islamic Republic's unjust and ruthless crackdown of peaceful dissent. Murdering political prisoners who are exercising their universal rights will not bring respect and legitimacy the Islamic Republic seeks. It will only serve to further isolate Iran's government in the world and from its people."

While the words are right, this is a shameful and totally inadequate response, intentionally articulated by a low-level White

House minion. The announcement, for all practical purposes inaudible, has no doubt once again reassured Tehran that the U.S. continues its policy of avoiding confrontation with the criminal regime. It certainly could have brought no encouragement to the hundreds of thousands of Iranians who, for the moment at least, have been beaten into submission.

As the presumed spokesman for America's vision of liberty and justice, the President has let us down as well.

Sunday, February 7, 2010

The Cost of War

A couple of weeks ago we began a determined (and frustrating) effort to try to make sense out of the U.S. military budget: in particular to try to isolate the cost of the Afghan war. There is no more depressing task.

We did this because the cost of the war should be as crucial a factor in the decision to fight as it is an examination of the validity of the Administration's assertion that we must "destroy al-Qaeda in Afghanistan." This is particularly the case since not one dollar of the cost is supported by Federal revenue: every buck represents pure deficit spending. Further, if the deficit is to be damned, I cannot help but think of the myriad ways the money could be spent in the U.S. for the common, long term good.

Regular readers will be well aware that for a variety of reasons (unconnected to dollar costs) I do NOT agree with the President's assertion that Afghanistan is a "necessary war." It seemed to me that an examination of the dollar cost of the war might support my point of view: I believe that it does - but readers will form their own opinion.

We have arrived at the following conclusions: (**Note**: All cost figures are in constant 2010 dollars.)

Department of Defense (DOD) Expenditures:

- The low point in post-Cold War military spending (i.e., before Iraq/Afghanistan) was $ 361 billion in 1998;

- The "base budget" (i.e., excluding wars) for 2010 is (about) $ 545 billion;

- Military spending in 2011 will be just over $700 billion, of which roughly $190 billion is applied to the cost of the wars in Iraq and Afghanistan.

- Spending, by comparison: Vietnam, 1966-1970 $495 billion; Cold War years, 1954-2001 $423 billion; 2011 $700 billion.

(Note: As far as we could determine from the Pentagon's arcane "Mexican bookkeeping," 2010 spending will be approximately the same or slightly lower than is budgeted for 2011.)

- The Congressional Budget Office (CBO) estimates the two-year cost of the additional 30,000 troops currently being deployed to Afghanistan to be about $30 billion, or $1 million per soldier. That cost, however, is NOT the full bill: the CBO also states that an additional $6 billion would probably be needed for this 30,000-man increment for the years 2012 and 2013: thus bringing the total cost of the additional 30,000 troops to $36 billion.

- The Iraq, and particularly the Afghan war, has been extraordinarily expensive when compared to previous conflicts. Looking at the cost per person per year (remember, in constant 2010 dollars): Korea: $393,000; Vietnam: $256,000; Iraq/Afghanistan: $459,000.

(**Note**: When the planned increase in troop strength in Afghanistan is completed, a conservative estimate is that the per person/per year cost for that war will rise to an absolutely astonishing $792,000.)

- The average per-person cost today is 78 percent higher than at the peak of the Reagan era; 95 percent higher than it was in 1989; and nearly three times the cost in the Vietnam era.

It is clear that Afghanistan - even considering the fairly low number of troops - is, and will continue to be, the most expensive war in U.S. history.

We must remember that the $190 billion price tag "formally" associated with Iraq/Afghanistan IS NOT a fair measure of the actual cost of our involvement in those wars. Much of the "baseline" budget will also go towards the cost of the wars - an invisible cost component.

Comment: the remarkably high dollar price of the war in Afghanistan is in many ways the result of a) logistics/transport costs that are nothing short of incredible; and b) the need to replace equipment that is unsuited to the kind of war we are bogged down in.

About $1.45 Trillion dollars was spent in military modernization in the 1991-2004 periods - basically to prepare the military to fight a conventional World War Three type war.

Much such spending went to procure "advanced" ground combat vehicles – many of which utterly failed in the counter-insurgency role they were forced to play in Iraq and Afghanistan. (Example: the "soft-skinned" Humvee. It took the Pentagon three years to acknowledge that these vehicles, purchased as part of the modernization program, were death traps when faced by the IED's and RPG's they confronted in counterinsurgency warfare. This has led to the design and on-going procurement of fleets of suitable vehicles like the MRAP - the Mine Resistant Ambush Protected vehicle.)

The Pentagon has been wary of increasing the actual number of full-time military personnel because of their virtually endless follow-on costs through the years, and uncertainty as to the length of the counterinsurgency wars. In fact, by the end of this calendar year the total number of full-time military personnel will be barely 50,000 more than it was at the post-Cold War low point, and about 22,000 of this number will in fact be "temporaries." Overall, the U.S. military is about 30 percent smaller than it was during the Cold War years.

This introduces the subject of "contractors" of various types, many of whom are hired to make up the shortfall in U.S. troops. In both Iraq and Afghanistan the numbers of contractors has exceeded the number of U.S. military personnel in country. U.S. Central Command stated (in late November 2009) that 104,100 contractors were employed in Afghanistan, at a time when U.S. combat forces numbered about 64,000.

According to CentCOM, the contractor breakdown is as follows:

Host country nationals (Afghans) 78,400

Third country nationals (not U.S.) 16,400

U.S. Citizens 9,300

Total 104,100

In December 2009 the Congressional Budget Office reported the following to Congress:

"Contractors make up 62 percent of DOD's "workforce" in Afghanistan. This is the highest recorded percentage of contractors used by DOD in any war in the history of the United States...

Assuming the same ratio of contractors-to-troops, deploying an additional 30,000 U.S. troops will require an additional 26,000 to 56,000 contractors."

CBO also reported that the U.S. military did not even begin to gather data on the contractors it hired until the second half on 2007, and stated that as of that time DOD's oversight of the entire contractor process was grossly inadequate.

The use of contractors is in many instances a good and cost effective idea, as in using locals as laborers on construction projects. There are, however, serious problems. For example, a significant number of Afghans have been hired and armed as local security guards. Since it is safe to assume that these people are easily recruited by the Taliban, the degree of "security" provided is doubtful at best. Knowing Afghans as I do, I for one would never employ them to "protect" me. These "guards" have also proven to be prone to violence against civilians.

Many Afghan contractors are employed in the movement of crucial supplies, particularly fuel, along the long road from Karachi, Pakistan to various sites in country. In fact, the entire fuel supply for our aircraft and vehicles in Afghanistan is dependent on thousands of hired Pakistani and Afghan trucks and drivers. Given the extraordinarily long and hazardous distance from the ONLY port in Pakistan, there is probably no way to eliminate this dangerous dependence on easily "converted" (to the Taliban) local helpers: but it means that our entire fuel "pipeline" is, essentially, already in enemy hands.

A very large percentage of U.S. citizen contractors are in fact "hired guns," thousands of whom actually serve to bolster the American presence on the ground without turning up on the list of U.S. combatants.

We could find NO information on the cost of these contractors. In fact CBO's exhaustive twenty-five page December 2009 report to Congress on the subject does not contain a single reference to cost – presumably because it is so buried in other budgets.

Our next article will look at the logistics nightmare in Afghanistan: a problem that both radically drives up the cost of our involvement and leaves U.S. dangeroU.S.ly vulnerable to insurgent attacks – and on the good will of other nations.

Hints: a gallon of gasoline, delivered to an operating base in Afghanistan, costs the U.S. taxpayer as much as $400. Every

American soldier based in the country must arrive and depart by air. Every vehicle, round of ammunition, weapon, or radio - pretty much everything that has a combat use - must come and go by air.

Sources of information on costs included: Congressional Research Service, Department of Defense Contractors in Iraq and Afghanistan: Background and Analysis, Dec 14, 2009; DOD New Article, Mullen Details What 2011 Budget Request will Fund, Feb 2, 2010; Project on Defense Alternatives, An Undisciplined Defense: Understanding the $2 Trillion Surge in U.S. Defense Spending, Jan 18, 2010; CBO Letter to Chairman of the Committee on the Budget, Jan 21, 2010; TPM Muckraker, How Many Private Contractors Are There in Afghanistan? Military Gives U.S. A Number, Dec 2, 2009; WSJ, Afghanistan Contractors Outnumber Troops, Aug 22, 2009.

Thursday, February 18, 2010

Iran: It Is Time to Act

From the U.S. perspective the situation in Iran has worsened considerably over the past year. First, the Iranian regime has repeatedly demonstrated that it will not only keep on developing nuclear weapons, but that it has increased the pace of its efforts. The same is true of its work developing effective ballistic missile delivery systems for those weapons. Second, the Iran's internal political situation is now totally unstable: the regime is now a military dictatorship with only a small vestige of clerical legitimacy. Iran's Revolutionary Guard is now more powerful than the clerical establishment, and I believe that it is safe to say that if the RG were to disappear tomorrow the entire Islamic structure of government would collapse in the wake of an immediate and successful country-wide popular uprising.

Note: For an eloquent discussion of Iranian unrest, the RG's power position in the country, and the cleric's loss of control, please see "Iran's Emerging Military Dictatorship" by Amir Taheri, WSJ, 16 February 2010.

The RG will not disappear. In fact, we can expect that it will continue to maintain and expand its stranglehold on the population and the clerical establishment. And, since it controls the nuclear program, it will continue to push that forward as fast as possible. Plus it will continue to subvert the democratic process in Iraq; build up the Hezbollah and Hamas terrorist organizations threatening Israel, and provide money and equipment to the Taliban.

Iran is vastly more important than Afghanistan. Developments in Iran will impact hugely on Iraq. In fact, they will determine whether the thin veneer of democratic government in that country, purchased with so much American blood and money, will or will not survive. And they will impact on the entire Middle East.

I believe President Obama is now - I repeat, now - at a point where he must decide whether he is prepared to accept and live with the inevitable emergence of a nuclear armed and highly unstable military dictatorship (with clerical trimmings to provide an aura of legitimacy) in Iran. OR that he cannot and that America must use its military power to destroy as much of Iran's nuclear infrastructure as possible; and to attack the coastal oil facilities without which Iran will suffer economic and government collapse.

In brief, Mr. Obama can choose to continue to temporize and vacillate over Iran, essentially letting the chips fall where they may, while continuing his focus on the endless, protracted and unwinnable war in Afghanistan (which does not matter one damn bit to America's strategic interests.) The enhanced "sanctions" which the President has ordered be designed (after a year of his failed "extended hand" policy) will NOT deter Iran, for the simple reason that China, Russia and others will neither agree to them nor honor them. "Sanctions' therefore, would be no more than another version of the "extended hand" - with equivalent results.

OR, the president can focus on the really tough, the really BIG problem: Iran. And decide that the U.S. must in its own interest (as well as in the interest of the cowardly nations who, while silently applauding our actions, will not stand by our side) bring down a military machine that oppresses the majority of its population and is determined to destabilize the Middle East.

If he opts to rely on sanctions, we will soon have a nuclear-armed Iran ruled by a fanatic military establishment (think Hitler's Gestapo and SS) with two primary goals: to continue to keep its population in submission, and to work in every possible way to destabilize the Middle East (meaning to work against U.S. interests.)

If he decides enough is enough, his only other option is to use military might to destroy at least a significant and crucial segment of Iran's nuclear establishment. Assuming he chooses that option, he should also decide to make selective surgical attacks on key oil export facilities, effectively cutting off Iran's national income. This will result in a collapsed economy and consequently failed government. It will give heart to the population, and lead to such massive uprisings that, as with the Shah, the Revolutionary Guard simply will not accept the burden of committing outright mass murder to keep its senior officers in power. The population, I now believe, wants to be rid of the Clerical regime, and more, important, its military masters.

There are a few helpful things on our side if he elects to use power. If Iran attempted to strike back - meaning at our forces in Iraq or the Gulf - we already have a huge and well-equipped army, naval and air presence in place, and many more assets in Afghanistan. These can and should be augmented by ordering a halt to all troop transfers out of Iraq, diverting forces slated for Afghanistan to Iraq, bringing in a couple of additional carrier battle groups; very publicly deploying additional stealth fighter and bomber aircraft closer to Iran, etc. No need to announce WHY... just do it.

Comment: This very public force realignment and augmentation will be seen by Tehran for what it is: a prelude to an American attack of unknown size and nature. It is highly unlikely but not impossible that these preparations may lead Tehran to accept the demand that all nuclear facilities be opened to international inspectors. If that happens, fine. If it does not, we have prepared ourselves to execute the necessary job of forcefully dealing with Iran.

Conclusion

Some months ago I wrote an article titled: "Nuclear Iran: Get Used to It," in which I concluded that we did not have a great deal of choice in the matter. Since then several things have happened to change my mind: First, the Iranian population has effectively voted against the regime and, I believe, now only needs a spark to set off a true people's revolution. Second: if there is any hope whatever of keeping Iraq on a democratic course Iran must be forced to end its subversive intervention. Third, I have no doubt that Israel, IF the U.S. does not act, will make a gallant but fundamentally impossible attempt to destroy Iran's nuclear "stuff." The consequences of that, I fear, would be greater and more adverse to our interests than doing the job ourselves. Fourth, If my assumptions that a) the mass of Iran's population want to be rid of the present regime, and b) that the selected attacks I describe above would provide the spark to revolution are correct, Iranians (unlike Iraqis) are sophisticated enough to set up a new working government in fairly short order. And Iran could be brought back to economic health fairly quickly. We are not talking about invading, occupying, and rebuilding a country.

Saturday, February 20, 2010

Iran vs. Obama

I wrote an article on 18 February 2010 urging the President to take direct military action against Iran. To my surprise, I found the following article, "Obama and Iran: Engagement has failed. The President needs a new strategy," in the 19 February Wall Street Journal, which, in the end, suggests that the President put the option of a "military strike" on the table. That greater minds than mine are turning in this direction is encouraging.

I want to focus on a fact that is generally not given sufficient weight when considering a military strike against Iran: such a strike must NOT be considered solely as a last-ditch effort to stop Iran's nuclear weapons program. It must also be viewed in the context of Iran's threat to Iraq's stability and, to a lesser extent, the prospects for Afghanistan. A key question is whether the President has this fact in mind as he continues his program of sanctions.

The survival of the fragile democracy in Iraq is, as a practical matter, entirely dependent on whether Iran is allowed to intervene - either by continued subversion or by direct military intervention after the U.S. departs. I believe that Iran's key near-term strategic objective, second only to the acquisition of nuclear weapons, is to dominate/control at least the southern two-thirds of Iraq. I believe that in order to accomplish this objective Iran already plans to shift from subversion to invasion, moving as soon as U.S. troops complete their withdrawal from Iraq.

One way or the other, Tehran intends to control Iraq after the U.S. leaves. Either the Administration is prepared to allow this, effectively throwing away progress dearly purchased by nearly ten years of war, thousands of American deaths, and untold billions of dollars. Or, the President must, by including the future of Iraq in his consideration of Iran's nuclear program, decide that he will not give Tehran the luxury of acting however it wishes in order to control Iraq.

The fact is that quite aside from the nuclear issue, the President will have to decide whether to deal militarily with this desperate and dangerous regime. There is simply no way the President can avoid facing a decision on initiating military action against Iran, and the sooner the issue is addressed the better. Face it now or face it later, but face it he must.

"Obama and Iran: Engagement has failed. The President needs a new strategy."

"These have been busy days for Iran's leadership. On January 28, the regime hanged two government opponents and sentenced 10 others to die. It has arrested and jailed some 500 opponents since December. Last week, it shut off access to Gmail and Google Buzz, as it already has done with Twitter, to prevent opposition forces from organizing. On the 31st anniversary of the Islamic Revolution, it jammed the streets of Tehran with supporters and security forces. Oh, and Mahmud Ahmadinejad announced that Iran has begun enriching uranium to 20% purity, making it a "nuclear state."

"Maybe now we can all agree that "engagement" with Iran has failed. So where does the Obama Administration go from here? It seems to be moving on multiple, not always coherent, fronts.

"Last Wednesday, the Treasury Department imposed sanctions on a commander of Iran's Revolutionary Guards Corps along with several IRGC-related companies said to be involved in WMD programs. And this week, Secretary of State Hillary Clinton warned that Iran may be evolving into a military dictatorship, with the Revolutionary Guards essentially running the show.

"The U.S. is also trying to get the U.N. Security Council to agree to a new round of sanctions on Iran, over continued Chinese opposition. A Western diplomatic source tells U.S. we can probably expect another essentially symbolic U.N. resolution in the coming weeks.

"Then there is Congress, which in the past two months has voted overwhelmingly for legislation that targets companies doing energy business with Iran. The two bills must now be reconciled, but the State

Department has previously sought to postpone the measures on grounds that they would constrain its room for diplomatic maneuver and could hurt the Iranian people.

"Our sources tell us the Administration may now reluctantly be willing to let Congress play bad cop as it pursues its sanctions options at the U.N. and, separately, with the Europeans. That's fine as far as it goes, and we hope the Administration understands that the Congressional bills would also have a major impact on the Revolutionary Guard, which dominates Iran's energy business and takes a huge cut from the $6 billion-plus annual gasoline trade, according to the Foundation for Defense of Democracies.

"Then again, we doubt even this Administration thinks that these sanctions alone can alter the regime's behavior, much less force its collapse. Instead—and in the absence of a credible threat of the use of U.S. military force—the Administration seems to be gambling its Iran policy on a set of assumptions that look increasingly wishful.

"One of these assumptions is that there may still be a "grand bargain" to be struck with the Iranian leadership, notwithstanding its refusals to do so last year amid President Obama's overtures. The Administration also allowed itself to imagine that Iran's protest movement would force the regime to take a more conciliatory nuclear line. It seems to have done the opposite.

"Another assumption is that Iran has encountered serious technical difficulties in its nuclear program, out of some combination of incompetence and perhaps sabotage. We certainly hope that's true. But the driving fact is that Iran seems to have repeatedly surmounted these obstacles over the years, and last year it surprised U.N. inspectors by producing more low-enriched uranium than anticipated. Enrichment only becomes easier as it moves to higher states of purity. And yesterday, the U.N. nuclear agency said it is worried that Iran may already be working on a nuclear warhead.

"Then there is the whispered assumption that a nuclear Iran would be "containable." But leaving aside the view that a religioU.S.ly fanatic regime can never safely be trusted with a bomb, a nuclear Iran would open the Pandora's box of nuclear proliferation in Saudi Arabia, Egypt and Turkey. For an Administration that has made nuclear nonproliferation a centerpiece of its agenda, allowing Iran to go nuclear would seem an odd way to advance that goal."

***

All of this suggests the need for a new U.S. strategy that drops the engagement illusion and begins to treat Iran as the single biggest threat to Mideast and U.S. security. Sanctions can be part of that strategy, but they will need to be more comprehensive than anything to date. They must also be ramped up rapidly because they will need time to be felt by the regime. The U.S. should give up on the U.N., which will only delay and dilute such pressure, and build a sanctions coalition of the willing.

The regime's recent crackdown suggests that the chances of regime change in the near term are remote, but popular animosity against Iran's rulers still seethes The U.S. can also speak and act far more forcefully and clearly on behalf of Iran's underground. The U.S. should assist that opposition in any way it can, especially with technology to help communicate with each other and the world.

Finally, the option of a military strike will have to be put squarely on the table. Sanctions have little chance of working unless they are backed by a credible military threat, and in any case Israel is more likely to act if it concludes that the U.S. won't. The risks of military action are obvious, but the danger to the world from a nuclear Iran is far worse.

After a year of lost time, Mr. Obama needs to put aside the diplomatic illusions of his campaign and make the hard decisions to stop the Revolutionary Guards.

Wednesday, February 24, 2010

Iraq: The Coming Crisis

Our national attention has been focused on Afghanistan for many months. Unfortunately, things have not been going well in Iraq, which is about to take center stage again.

While Joe Biden recently commented that Iraq was one of the Obama Administration's "successes," the fact is that we are quickly approaching the most dangerous and difficult period in our long, unhappy involvement in that country: elections and the attempt to create a National Government.

Iraq will hold national elections in less than two weeks, and thereafter attempt to create a national government which, we hope, will give the country a modicum of democracy; balance and accommodate wildly antagonistic regional and religious differences; settle major internal economic issues (i.e., how is oil revenue shared); and provide an acceptably stable internal security situation.

Iraq is to do this against a backdrop of radical reductions in U.S. military presence: under the 2008 Status of Forces agreement with the Iraqi Government we are to have withdrawn virtually all of our combat units by the end of this August, leaving a largely non-combatant residual force of 50,000 to "support Iraqi Security forces." Initial plans were to have drawn our force level in Iraq down to 115,000 by now. In fact, we have moved more quickly, and only about 96,000 troops remain. Ten thousand U.S. soldiers a month are to start leaving Iraq in a matter of weeks.

Even if the elections themselves go fairly well, the record of the past five or six years of political chaos and sectarian violence in Iraq is dismal. Only the most determined optimist could believe that there is a chance that the new National Assembly can meet the above goals. As a start in complicating matters, last weekend the leading Sunni minority party withdrew from the elections completely. And we can be certain that covert Iranian support for the Shia - and for disruption in general - will increase as our troop levels drop.

Unlike Afghanistan, the condition that Iraq is in when we leave really matters. It is not just an internal game that the Iraqis will be playing in the next months: Iran is a determined player and can be relied upon to do its utmost to influence events in its favor. I think that civil war in Iraq seems very likely – probably starting well before the remainder of our non-combatant units have left at the end of 2011.

One can run various scenarios on developments in Iraq - starting now, and moving forward just a year or two - that range from the hugely optimistic "all will be well" to flat out Iranian invasion. What is very likely is that the Administration is soon going to have to make serious decisions: decisions that I suspect will boil down to whether the U.S. will or will not walk away from a failed Iraq. We must hope that the White House and Pentagon are already playing a serious game of "What if."

Friday, March 19, 2010

In the Wake of the Marja Offensive

The "Marja Offensive" in Helmand Province has been widely advertised by U.S. commanders as the "new model" for counter-insurgency fighting in Afghanistan. We are all familiar with the concept: provide advance warning to the local Taliban so that they can withdraw from the area, thus reducing casualties to our troops, the Taliban and resident civilians; inject large numbers of U.S. and British troops - accompanied by equally large numbers of the New Afghan Army - to take and hold a carefully defined area; install an imported "ready-made" Afghan local government; and, finally, provide jobs for the locals.

This "package" of measures, the U.S. high command believes, will enable the Afghan Government to establish real control over the area, and, once duplicated in other locations, is the way to drive out the Taliban while establishing and maintaining Afghan Government control over ever-larger areas of the country.

While certainly an improvement over simply attacking Taliban forces in an area and then leaving, I was of the opinion from the outset that, sadly, the new concept would NOT work. And cannot work in other areas. My opinion is based on my years of involvement with the Afghan insurgency against the Soviets, and what I think is a decent appreciation of how things work in Afghanistan.

I have refrained from commenting on the strategy until we had reliable information on how the concept was actually working. On the strictly "military" side of things, it quickly became evident that even after warning the Taliban away from the area and deploying overwhelming troop strength (plus extensive air and artillery support), simply occupying the ground was not an easy task. Our casualties were low since, as I expected, only a limited number of Taliban fighters remained to contest the offensive, however, enough fighters remained to significantly slow down our movement, inflict casualties, and demonstrate that they were NOT going to abandon the ground. Even this very limited resistance cost us lives and wore down our troops: i.e., it was a much tougher job than had been anticipated. On top of this the Taliban's deployment of extraordinary numbers of IED's greatly hampered our movements - and increased our casualties.

Comment: This IED deployment, exactly along the routes we had to take, made a mockery of claims by many U.S. officers that our extensive air surveillance and interdiction capabilities, both day and night, robbed the Taliban of the ability to place large numbers of IED's in our way.

I have seen no repeat no reporting on how the New Afghan Army performed in the offensive. Given that prior to the operation much emphasis was placed on the assertion that this was a "joint" Afghan-NATO operation - in effect a demonstration of our success in creating an Afghan Army - this silence strongly suggests that the Afghans did not perform well.

If that is the case we are deliberately being denied a "report card" on the Afghan troops. This is understandable only if the Afghans did badly, since the Administration's justification for expanding our presence was and is that the New Afghan Army will be able to take over from U.S. in very short order. Absent news to the contrary, I suspect that the Afghan Army's performance was not what was expected, and casts very severe doubts on the Administration's assertions. It has long been my view that creating an effective Afghan Army is, as a practical matter, impossible. I can only wonder if that was demonstrated in the Marja offensive.

My biggest concern during the build-up for the offensive was - and is - that I do not accept the validity of the strategy. Briefly stated, the Taliban's willingness to use terror to intimidate and coerce the population, plus the inability of the Afghan Government to field an effective and loyal Army, will defeat our efforts.

Wednesday, May 26, 2010

Intelligence Analysis: Afghanistan Strategy Doomed to Failure

Summary

The "new model" counterinsurgency strategy now underway in Afghanistan, supported by steadily increasing numbers of U.S. military personnel, is doomed to fail. This is the result of the Taliban's countering the strategy by the highly effective use of terror tactics against the Afghan population, and of NATO's inability to field adequate numbers of trained and loyal Afghan military and police. There is no evidence that the Taliban is weakening: on the contrary, over the past months the Taliban has staged a number of attacks on both civilian and military targets around the country.

Discussion

General McChrystal's highly touted "new" counterinsurgency strategy is a fairly simple one. First, place a large number of NATO and Afghan troops in a carefully selected area, thus by sheer force of numbers denying the Taliban the ability to operate openly in any strength. Second, introduce sufficient numbers of Afghan military, police, and civilian administrators to demonstrate that the "government" is on hand, and is capable (backed up by NATO forces) of both rooting out Taliban supporters and protecting the local population from the Taliban - long term. Third, provide assistance, in cash or kind, to the local population to, in effect, buy their support. Fourth, work to wean Taliban supporters to the "government" side.

The first test of this strategy was in the Marja area this past spring. *(Please see my article, dated 19 March 2010, on that offensive.)* The results have not been promising. For example, the Taliban has successfully dissuaded farmers from accepting irrigation pumps (an important part of a multi-million dollar "inducement" package) by simply killing the first farmers who accepted them. Only a handful of locals have accepted employment in aid projects - out of more than a thousand jobs offered - because the Taliban has passed the word that accepting employment would result in death. Taliban attacks and intimidation have essentially stalled construction and employment projects. And virtually no progress has been made in identifying, capturing, or killing the many Taliban in the area.

The second, and vastly more ambitious, operation is now underway: an effort to take control of the very heartland of the Taliban - Kandahar city and its environs.

The reinforcements that Gen. McChrystal called for last summer are pouring into the country: there are now more U.S. troops, nearly 100,000, in Afghanistan than there are in Iraq, and many more will soon arrive as our withdrawal from Iraq is completed in the next few months.

The strategy is conceptually sound, and, I believe, the best that could be designed. Highly experienced, motivated, trained and well equipped U.S. and British troops are deploying in the area, as are a (very limited) number of Afghan civil/military/police forces. Thus a comprehensive strategy which combines force with inducements - and the promise of long-term effective government - is being set in motion.

While the U.S./NATO strategy is the best that could be devised, its success depends on the assumption that the enemy against which it is employed conducts its activities within certain norms of civilized behavior. The strategy will fail, because the Taliban, operating outside the bounds of such behavior, has devised and is using a counter-strategy that our forces cannot effectively retaliate against and defeat.

That strategy is the use of terror and violence, real and threatened, against the civilian population.

This is a simple strategy that does not involve major attacks on U.S./NATO forces, which the Taliban knows it cannot risk or win. It relies instead on the assassination, carried out by Taliban elements buried in the population, of locals who support or cooperate with U.S. and the so-called Afghan Government. Briefly put, locals who support or cooperate with U.S. are killed. The price of cooperation with U.S., therefore, is death.

There are a number of reasons why the Taliban strategy will work.

There is not an Afghan alive, Taliban or not, who believes that the U.S./NATO is in Afghanistan for the long haul. Quite the opposite - the Americans have declared their intention to leave. Whether their departure is in one or two or three years is irrelevant: they are going, and going "soon." Their departure will remove the only effective defense against the Taliban.

Thus every local, for whom long term survival is THE key issue, must look to the near future when deciding whether to support the Americans (who are leaving) and the nominal Afghan central government (which is an ineffective and corrupt fiction, propped up only by the Americans) OR to accede to the Taliban. Given that equation, only a fool would cast his lot with NATO/Kabul.

Particularly when, in the present period before the U.S. departure and the central government's collapse, one knows that the Taliban can and will kill those who cooperate with the Americans.

Why risk death at the hands of the Taliban when they will prevail in the end?

President Obama's decision to remain in AND expand the war in Afghanistan was, we are told, based on the premise that by temporarily increasing both our troop strength and aid levels we would buy time to train and deploy large numbers of Afghan military, police and civil government personnel - who would then be able to deal with the Taliban themselves. As I forecast at the time, this has proven impossible. For myriad reasons those resources have NOT materialized. Nor, I believe, will they. Thus whatever "control" is exercised over a selected area by joint NATO-Afghan forces is actually only the result of the NATO input: once that is withdrawn, the Afghan element will simply fail.

Conclusions

I believe that in the coming months the Kandahar operation, designed to be the model for all in-country NATO activity, will result in the following situation:

The large NATO military presence will give the illusion that NATO and the (so-called) Afghan Government "controls" the area. Taliban influence and dominance will, however, NOT be destroyed.

Taliban activity - the "terror strategy" - will continue, and will successfully frustrate our efforts to eradicate the Taliban, install effective civil government, and establish effective aid programs.

At the same time the Taliban will continue to attack NATO and Afghan Government targets around the country. U.S. and NATO forces will continue to take casualties - although not at the same levels that we saw when the basic U.S. policy was to seek out and engage Taliban units.

As a practical matter, this situation can and will drag on indefinitely. There is no silver bullet, no combination of force and economic inducement that can defeat an enemy that operates with deadly inhumanity in the midst of a war-weary population.

At what point does the President come to realize that the "new" counter-insurgency strategy, supported by massive troop increases and aid programs, does not and will not work?

Biography

Howard P. Hart was an officer in CIA's Clandestine Service - the Agency's espionage arm – during the Cold War. His primary intelligence specialties during these years were Soviet military weaponry, counter-terrorism, and weapons of mass destruction.

He attended Cornell University and the University of Arizona, and has both B.A. and M.A. degrees in Oriental Studies and Political Science. His languages include Hindustani/Urdu, Indonesian and German.

Made in the USA
Lexington, KY
11 May 2017